SEASONS OF THANKS

SEASONS OF THANKS

Graces and Blessings for Every Home

Taz Tagore

STEWART, TABORI & CHANG
NEW YORK

Published in 2005 by
Stewart, Tabori & Chang
115 West 18th Street
New York, NY 10011
www.abramsbooks.com

Library of Congress Cataloging-in-Publication Data

Tagore, Taz.
Seasons of thanks : graces and blessings for every home / Taz Tagore.
p. cm.
Includes bibliographical references.
ISBN 1-58479-429-1
1. Prayers. 2. Grace at meals. 3. Benediction. 4. Blessing and cursing. I. Title.

BL560.T34 2005
204'.33—dc22

2005007644

Designed by Julie Hoffer

The text of this book was composed in Humanist and Lord Swash.

Printed in China

10 9 8 7 6 5 4 3 2 1
First Printing

Stewart, Tabori & Chang is a subsidiary of

LA MARTINIÈRE
GROUPE

ACKNOWLEDGMENTS

May all those who carefully read and edited,
who eagerly brainstormed and gently instructed,
who generously supported and lovingly counseled,
be blessed for your infinite patience and joyful participation:
Shafana, Shamash, and Adam;
Jennifer, Stephanie, Alison, Corey, and Niko;
Lisa, Alvin, Harry, Renee, Jeff, and Thoryn;
Ed, Judith, Cindi, Laura, and bell—
may you consider this book to be a part of you,
and a part of us.

CONTENTS

INTRODUCTION

Every one of us is a mystic. We may or may not realize it; we may not even like it. But whether we know it or not, whether we accept it or not, mystical experience is always there, inviting us on a journey of ultimate discovery.
—Wayne Teasdale, *The Mystic Heart*

I have always loved words. As a child, I spent hours poring over the dictionary, hunting down new, unfamiliar, and mysterious words. During my early love affair with the dictionary, I encountered the word *gratefulness*. In my mind, it was a mouthful of consonants that evoked either Tony the Tiger roaring about Frosted Flakes or having to thank my great-aunt for giving me yet another pair of itchy woolen socks for my birthday. It seemed like a word I could live without.

Nearly two decades later, I have written a book about living gratefully. I wanted to detail the small but special moments—seasonal changes, annual holidays, and personal rituals—that breathe life into every month of the year. My hope is that they will add up to the difference between a year half-empty and a year half-full. The accompanying blessings, poems, songs, quotes, and excerpts are intended to inspire readers to express gratefulness alone or with others, at mealtimes or at any time of day. *Seasons of Thanks* is about awakening to the subtle beauty, wisdom, and joy that inhabits every moment of our lives.

Many people have asked how I made the leap from blissful ignorance of gratefulness and its meaning to writing an entire book about it. Thankfully, being awakened to the goodness in life is not a result of one's genetic disposition or initiation into a secret society of thanks-givers. Gratefulness—a conviction, an outlook, and a daily practice—is available to everyone. Some are born ready to view the world through the lens of appreciation.

For others, the moment of awakening arrives after feeling restless or taking life for granted. Although my personal experience resembles the latter, the destination is delightful, regardless of the path taken.

For me, becoming a more grateful person has led to personal transformation; some changes are largely invisible, while others are readily apparent to my friends, colleagues, and family. For example, I rarely sit down to a meal without reciting a prayer of thanks. This small gesture, practiced nearly every day, has amounted to a radical change in my life. Today, I am a more content and generous person because I have learned how to give thanks.

Gratefulness has also shaped my professional life. I recently left a corporate career to start the Reciprocity Foundation—a nonprofit that helps creative homeless youth gain the mentorship and skills to become interior, fashion, product, and graphic designers. The nonprofit sister organization—a social enterprise called the Appreciate Network—helps people express appreciation with thoughtful sentiments, stories, and gifts. The organization's website (www.appreciate.org) is fast becoming *the* online destination for gifts made by socially responsible companies and packaged by creative homeless youth. We like to say that we sell "double-wrapped gifts"—gifts that express a heartfelt sentiment and help others share their gifts with the world: A portion of the proceeds I receive from this book will be donated to the Reciprocity Foundation to fund programs focused on the twin goals of nurturing creative expression and appreciation in our communities.

Learning to appreciate others and oneself is not a trivial undertaking and only recently became a way of life for me. For most of my life, I thought I was an appreciative person because I frequently said "thank you." But I didn't slow down long enough to understand or experience gratefulness. By my late twenties, I had been elected president of my undergraduate students' association, worked at an elite consulting firm, written and directed several plays, started a national young feminist group, volunteered at Mother Teresa's hospice in Calcutta, traveled the world, and earned an MBA from the Harvard Business School. My life had acquired the metallic sheen of success; I worked so hard and on so many different projects that I barely had time to appreciate the wonderful people and moments in my life. Feeling disconnected from myself, I signed up for a ten-day meditation retreat in western Massachusetts that began the day after I finished business school.

The retreat was like nothing I had experienced before. Upon entering, I signed a contract agreeing not to talk, read, listen to music, write, or acknowledge others (even still, I snuck in a notebook and ballpoint pen). Stripped of my accomplishments and status, I felt truly alone. I sat in meditation for eight hours a day, ate sparingly, took short walks, and slept as though my life depended on it. Even though I had a bed, three square meals a day, and plenty of time to reflect, I couldn't enjoy the the silence. Seven days passed without incident. Then it happened.

I was seated at the end of a long table, eating porridge and drinking tea. The food, venue, and scenery were utterly unremarkable. In fact, I was on the verge of engaging in an internal dialogue about how bored and dissatisfied I was when—for no apparent reason—I stopped. In that moment, I looked down at my plain breakfast, the bare concrete floor, my faded pajamas, and the overcast sky and was flooded with a gorgeous, life-affirming energy. My body tingled. My senses awakened. My heart pounded, bursting with emotion. Suddenly, everything seemed different. My porridge turned into a bowl of hearty oats and plump raisins drizzled with honey. My cup of tea became a warm, soothing elixir. The clouds glowed with the radiant energy of the sun. Instead of feeling dissatisfied, I embraced the quiet beauty of the moment. In an instant, my entire perspective had changed.

When an older woman nearby bowed her head and softly recited a blessing, I watched her, entranced. Without thinking, I too bowed my head and recited a prayer of gratitude. I can't remember what I said or whom I thanked but, in that moment, everything came naturally. Several decades after finding the word in the dictionary, I finally understood its meaning. Gratefulness is a moment when you understand, with all your being, that you are truly blessed.

When I returned to Cambridge, I couldn't contain my curiosity about *gratefulness* and saying grace. I wanted to understand how and when gratefulness became a part of the human vocabulary—I wanted to understand how a simple word could have such a profound impact on a person's life.

Some historians give credit for saying grace to the Romans but the practice has been traced back to hunter-gatherers who are believed to have blessed their food because a full meal was so rare. As we evolved, so too did our ability to emote. When food was scarce, we beseeched the sun, sky, and earth gods with prayers and rituals. When food was plentiful, we sang and danced our thanks. These ceremonies were the earliest manifestations of grateful behavior.

Charles Panati, author of *Extraordinary Origins of Everyday Things*, suggests that our prayers evolved after we began to cultivate the earth. He writes, "After the dawn of agriculture, civilization's first farmers began to pray to their gods for bountiful harvests." Organized religion encouraged followers to say grace. Jews created the Brachot—a collection of Hebrew blessings for bread, wine, fruit, meat—nearly every imaginable food item. The practice also spread to other religions; observant Christians and Muslims began reciting blessings of thanks before meals.

Today, nearly every religious and cultural group has developed its own tradition for expressing gratitude. While religion is often a source of divisiveness among people, saying grace is a unifying ritual. In Asia, I observed Buddhist monks making a food offering to Buddha and blessing the meal; in Africa, I heard songs of gratitude echo from drums, feet, and throats; in Europe, I watched families bow their heads, fold their hands, and recite a simple prayer; in North America, I witnessed so many different variations of grace that I lost count. A 1997 Gallup Poll reported that approximately 80 percent of Americans occasionally or frequently recite grace at mealtimes. I have met people who pray before every meal, every snack (even a candy bar!), and who pray before and after a meal. I have since concluded that the impulse to offer thanks is universal—only our expressions of it vary from place to place.

This phenomenon was in part explained by the American yogi Judith Hanson Lasater when she said, "Grace is the substratum of everything in the universe. It is our choice whether or not to embrace it." Dr. Lasater explained that we are, and have always been, the recipients of too many "things"—food, water, protection, and so on—that we simply cannot attribute to human effort or ingenuity. Even still, many of us struggle to acknowledge our blessings—some are too busy to notice, some feel undeserving, and some fear acknowledging their dependence on others. Learning to reconcile these fears is an essential part of living gratefully.

The word *grace* is etymologically derived from the Latin word *gratia*, meaning thanks or favor, and originally described the gifts bestowed by a loving and generous creator. Early Jews and Romans recited grace to acknowledge "gifts from God" and the work of "God's grace." Saying grace is a means of joyfully acknowledging our dependence on others and a higher power for our survival. It is true that we depend on the earth, the sun, and the labor of farmers, construction workers, doctors, business managers, chemists, and so on to fulfill our basic needs. In return, we must strike a balance between needing and being needed, giving and expressing appreciation.

On the silent retreat, I awakened to the joy of eating a simple breakfast. The experience taught me that I needn't seek out opportunities to be grateful—they exist everywhere. For those who awaken to gratefulness, the simple act of living serves as sufficient inspiration to recognize goodness and express thanks.

Ram Dass, a contemporary spiritual leader, was quoted as saying that "whatever comes along—death, life, joy, sadness—is grist for the mill of awakening." While it is easy to be grateful for a terrific meal or a pleasurable experience, it is much harder to be grateful for something that causes pain. Without the benefit of hindsight, it is difficult to find the joy in a failing grade or a lapsed relationship. However, living gratefully invites us to believe that some good will be born out of every experience. It can take weeks, months, or even years to appreciate our past struggles. However, it is important to learn how to accept and be grateful for everything in our lives—both good and bad.

Like strengthening a muscle, the capacity for gratefulness requires practice. For me, saying grace is a simple way to do this. It has become one of the most important and recurrent rituals in my life. Saying grace is the perfect spiritual snack—easy to prepare and share, quick, portable, and deeply satisfying. It also occurs alongside one of the most pleasurable experiences in my life: eating!

Saying grace is a simple but profound ritual. It unites the experience of consuming food, which sustains life, and the experience of expressing appreciation, which inspires us to embrace life. Perhaps that is why it is practiced throughout the world: Saying grace simultaneously strums the chords underlying the mind, body, and spirit.

Food, or the mere anticipation of it, serves as strong inspiration to say grace. The aroma, texture, color, flavor, and arrangement delight my senses. When a plate of food is placed in front of me, it is the only time when I inhale deeply and prepare for a truly sensorial experience. Biologists have discovered that the metabolism of the whole body shifts in anticipation of a meal. The sight or fragrance of food causes a dilation of pupils, an increase in heart rate, and the secretion of saliva and gastric and pancreatic juices from digestive organs. All these changes can occur even before the actual ingestion of food! I often plan my meals in advance and catch myself daydreaming about what I'll have for dinner. When I finally sit down to eat, I can't help but offer thanks to the earth for the raw ingredients, to local farmers for coaxing it out of the earth, and to the chef (usually me!) who prepared the meal. In my view, it is difficult not to be grateful for food.

Saying grace also begets empathy for the suffering caused by the absence of food. While America produces more than enough food for its population and much of the rest of the world, millions of Americans suffer from malnutrition or hunger. Knowledge of the global hunger crisis affects my experiences with food. Sometimes I feel guilty sitting down to a large meal, particularly during the holidays. On these occasions, I am reminded that it is a privilege to enjoy three meals a day. Only rarely do I experience a hunger pang that cannot immediately be satisfied. Saying grace reinforces the idea that I shouldn't take even a simple meal for granted.

Nancy, a woman I met at a bridal shower, reminded me that saying grace is also an important rite of passage for many people. Nancy had her first public speaking experience at the dinner table—her mother invited her to say grace at a family gathering. She practiced her mother's favorite blessing until she could recite it perfectly. After her dinnertime debut, everyone at the table clapped and cheered her efforts. As Nancy grew more confident, she wrote her own blessings and recited spontaneous prayers of thanks. Eventually, her self-confidence seeped into other parts of her life; she became more articulate in class and at social events. Nancy's experience suggests that saying grace is a ritual that inspires self-assurance at the dinner table and beyond.

For many, mealtimes are a rare and much-needed opportunity to take a break. Nowadays, many people eat "on the run" and don't even bother to sit down during meals. One translation of the biblical phrase "to pray" is to come to rest. Saying grace is a ritual that helps me transition from the working day into a state of serenity. Holding hands, closing one's eyes, and ceasing conversation all have a calming effect, especially in the midst of our fast-paced lives. After saying grace, I feel more centered and clear-headed.

Sometimes after a particularly stressful or challenging day, I find it difficult to feel or express appreciation. Saying grace, like any other sacred ritual, requires preparation. Many religious texts call for physical or spiritual ablution before prayer—Muslims wash their hands and feet before entering a mosque. Many church, synagogue, mosque, and temple services invite congregants to sing or chant before reciting an important prayer. My friend Kevin always closes his eyes and takes a deep breath before saying grace. Ronald Fry, a professor at Case Western Reserve University, invites his wife and son to describe one positive event in their day before the evening meal. Saying grace works best when it is viewed as more than a barrier between hunger and satiation. After taking a short walk or sitting quietly, I can focus my attention on describing something—large or small—for which I am thankful.

Saying grace can translate into noticeable changes in the way we experience and respond to life. Sometimes after saying grace, I notice that little details work themselves out. My sister maintains that her daughter is always more aware and playful after prayer. Others believe that assuming a posture of gratefulness leads to more and more blessings. Practicing this heartfelt ritual is one way to stop and focus on what is good in our lives—it is a moment that invites us to celebrate, rather than complain about, being human.

Now, several years after reciting my first blessing, I say thanks whenever and wherever I am struck with a feeling of gratitude. I always try to do it in a way that reflects the unique experiences of the day, the season, and the people with whom I am sharing the meal. I also practice this ritual when I am dining alone—it brings a greater level of enjoyment and awareness to an otherwise quiet meal. I have collected stacks of books filled with prayers, songs, and stories from different regions of the world. Before celebrating a family birthday or holiday, I search my collection for the perfect blessing. Sometimes I use the Internet or local library to help me find a heartwarming Christian prayer or African praise song to preface the meal; alternately, I invite everyone to partake in a moment of silence. *Seasons of Thanks* is intended to make the process of finding and sharing a suitable blessing a little easier.

Like a trusted cookbook that has become an essential part of preparing and sharing the evening meal, I hope this book earns a central place at the dinner table. Before sitting down to a meal, invite someone to read the anecdotes and historical facts associated with a particular holiday or season. It is a simple way to create a feeling of communion. After everyone is seated and the food has been served, reciting a blessing from the book will amplify the goodwill and warmth of the gathering. At dinner parties, I'll share a story or blessing with a group of friendly or unfamiliar faces—it is a great way to break the ice and stimulate conversation. With any luck, *Seasons of Thanks* will soon begin to show signs of healthy aging—pages softened by the touch of many hands and a spine stretched from all the page markers and notes stuffed inside.

The essays in the book—describing the holidays, rituals, and seasonal changes in every month of the year—are intended to evoke the spirit of each month and to connect everyday events with a feeling of gratefulness. As it turns out, nearly every culture and religion celebrates the arrival of spring, the harvest season, holy days, and days of remembrance. *Seasons of Thanks* honors the common ritualistic ground shared by people from all walks of life.

Some of the seasonal holidays, rituals, and foods described in the book may reflect your own family traditions—others will be unfamiliar. As such, you might use this book to celebrate rituals practiced in a far-away place or to invent new rituals—if only to spice up an otherwise uneventful day or month! Having been raised in snowy Canada, I always wished for a holiday to celebrate the first snowfall. Last year, I decided not to wait any longer. When I awoke to a winter-white landscape, I planned a spontaneous gathering with a few close friends. Throughout the meal, we read winter poetry, sang Christmas carols, and recited joyful blessings. I hope you will be inspired to create and celebrate the holidays that you always wished for.

Most of the holidays and rituals in the book are accompanied by blessings. They were culled from saints, philosophers, poets, writers, songwriters, mystics, politicians, artists, and everyday people. Some were written more than a thousand years ago, and others were birthed just before this book went to print. Similar subjects and themes underlie all the blessings, regardless of when or by whom they were composed. I encourage you to read, sing, or dramatize them to suit your tastes. Many of the blessings included have become staples at my dinner table; I hope you too will cultivate a short list of beloved blessings—ones that ring true in your heart and communicate something new with every reading.

Finally, I hope that this book is a milestone on your journey to live a grateful life. Once you've uncovered it, gratefulness is hard to contain. Learning how to say grace inspired me to write this book; writing this book awakened me to the blessings in my life, which in turn inspired me to start a nonprofit that appreciates and helps those in need. Brother David Steindl-Rast, a Benedictine monk and author of the book *Gratefulness, the Heart of Prayer,* eloquently described the process of living gratefully:

As I express my gratitude, I become more deeply aware of it. And the greater my awareness, the greater my need to express it. What happens here is a spiraling ascent, a process of growth in ever expanding circles around a steady center, a movement leading ever more deeply into gratefulness.

Writing this book has deepened my understanding of and capacity to appreciate—both in word and in deed. Now it's your turn. Turn the page, open your heart, and pass it on.

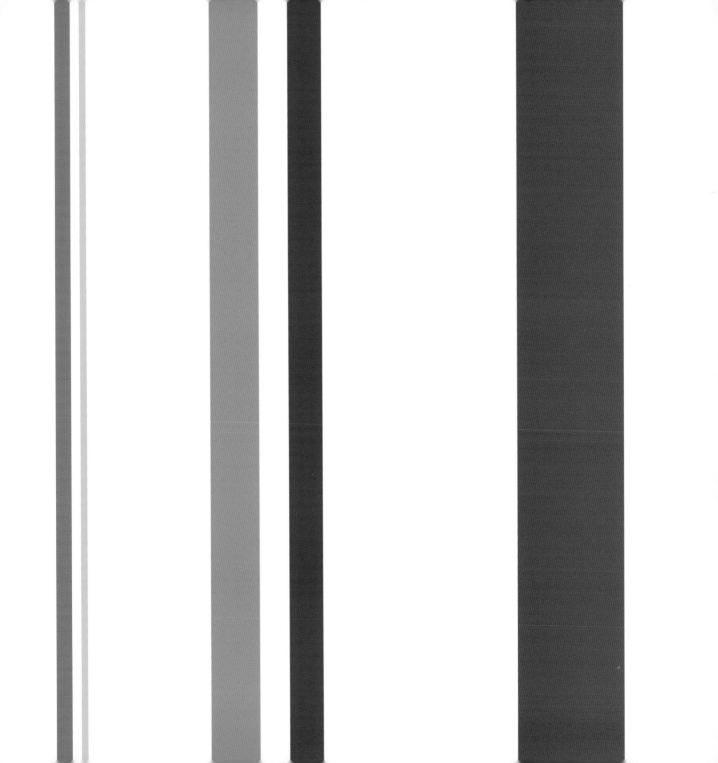

Labor Day
Rosh Hashanah
Yom Kippur
Diwali
Halloween
Thanksgiving

Autumn

SEPTEMBER: *Gaining Wisdom and Strength*

September is a twilight month between the seasons—a moment when the air is filled with a mixture of summer and fall. If our engines were idling in August, we move them into high gear in September, a month forever associated with learning, inside and outside of the classroom. It is a time of discovery, a season of awakening to new ideas and philosophies. In September, we strive to experience the world in new ways.

Hold on to what is good,
Even if it is a handful of earth.
Hold on to what you believe,
Even if it is a tree which stands by itself.
Hold on to what you must do,
Even if it is a long way from here.
Hold on to life,
Even when it is easier letting go.
Hold on to my hand,
Even when I have gone away from you.
—Traditional, Pueblo

August's humidity dissipates into warm September afternoons and perfect autumn evenings. During the day, the skies are peppered with monarch butterflies gracefully sipping milkweed nectar on their winter migration route. Broad-winged hawks soar through the air, powered by September's strong thermal air currents. Below them, vast stretches of farmland are filled with pale wheat and golden ears of corn. Forested areas unveil early splashes of gold, bronze, and red—a color palette evoking life rather than decomposition.

Golden yellow school buses materialize from the early morning mist to pick up clusters of schoolchildren eagerly chatting about the summer holidays. The buses plod through their routes—stopping and starting, over and over—their doors clumsily swinging open to engulf another batch of youngsters. Children, sporting brand-new knapsacks and sneakers, reunite with old friends and size up new students at the school. Schoolyards are instantly invigorated and resemble a grand bazaar:

lunches, toys, sporting cards, and stories are heavily traded during recess and lunch hour. September 8 is **International Literacy Day**, a day honoring the joys of being able to read and write.

Inside office buildings and skyscrapers, similar patterns emerge. Lunchrooms, cafeterias, and favorite takeout destinations that were empty in August are now filled with office workers shouting orders and clamoring for a table. Telephones ring with greater frequency, and printers are clogged by the fresh demand for documents. New teams and committees are formed to tackle business challenges with renewed vigor. Calendars fill up with appointments that couldn't be scheduled in July and August. Commutes to and from the office serve as welcome respites during which to review to-do lists, contracts, and research reports. Like the schoolyards in our neighborhoods, our workplaces spring into action in September.

Labor Day, the last holiday of the summer season, is celebrated on the first Monday of September. Peter McGuire organized the first Labor Day in September 1882 to honor workers in the factories, offices, and streets of New York City. Eventually, it became a day on which to recognize the contributions of middle-class workers to the economy. In the early twentieth century, it also became a national holiday in Canada. On this day, workers are honored with special parades in the streets and special prayers inside halls of worship. And, most important, they are given a day off work!

Today, Labor Day marks the last long weekend of the summer. For some, it is a time to close up the vacation home by stowing lawn furniture, outdoor games, or closing the pool. For

And I learned that I lived
Always and everywhere.
I learned that I knew everything,
Only I had forgotten.
I learned that I grew,
Only I had overlooked things.
Now I am back, remembering.
—"Song of Return," Dagara Tribe

Lord, be with me in my career.
Guide my temper and my speech,
And the things that make me laugh.
Help me never to be lazy
Or do my job by half.
May God be reflected in me
By those that I affect.
Let me treat my fellow workers
With kindness and respect.
—Christian Worker's Prayer

Be generous in prosperity, and thankful in adversity.
Be a lamp unto those who walk in darkness, and a home to the stranger.
Be a breath of life on the body of humankind, dew to the soil of the human heart, and
a fruit upon the tree of humility.
—From a Baha'i Prayer for Peace

the fashion-conscious, Labor Day is the last weekend to wear white clothing. For fans of sports and politics, it marks the beginning of intense political campaigning in an election year, the beginning of the football season, and the start of the "September stretch," a series of final baseball games that culminate in the World Series.

In September, the harvest gains momentum. Golden ears of corn and fleshy squash fill roadside stands and farmers' markets. The Algonquin, Cree, and Ojibwa peoples begin to harvest wild rice from shallow lakes. Some tribes mount festivals or prepare special meals to taste the first fruits of the season.

On **September 11**, we honor the tragic loss of civilians, firefighters, and emergency workers after the terrorist attacks on the World Trade Center in New York City in 2001. St. Paul's Chapel, located adjacent to Ground Zero, serves as a reminder of the hope and community that was born out of this tragedy. For months afterward, volunteers from across the country donated time and energy to support rescue workers and to restore the spirit of lower Manhattan. In honor of the people who

I dream a world where man
No other man will scorn,
Where love will bless the earth
And peace its paths adorn.
—From "I Dream a World," Langston Hughes

passed away and those who offered hope and healing to the victims, we recite prayers of peace on this day.

Around September 21, the **Autumnal Equinox**, the sun rises directly in the east and sets directly in the west. In equatorial countries, the sun passes directly overhead so that no shadows are created! For some people, the last quarter of the year arouses bittersweet feelings. As the sun slips beneath the horizon earlier and earlier, we challenge ourselves to find light in the dark quarter of the year.

All Jewish holidays are considered holy days, but **Rosh Hashanah** and **Yom Kippur** are the most sacred or "high" holidays. Rosh Hashanah is the first day of the Jewish calendar and is a joyous celebration. An ancient Hebrew tradition involves visiting a body of water on Rosh Hashanah to recite the Tashlich prayer and shaking one's clothing as though tossing accumulated sins into the water. On the eve of Rosh Hashanah, Jews attend synagogue and then return home for a festive meal with their families. On the following day, an extra prayer service (in addition to the traditional thrice-daily prayers) is performed at synagogue. The evening meal is comprised of sweet foods, such as ripe apples and challah dipped in honey, to evoke the joy of the year that has just passed. Some families celebrate Rosh Hashanah by taking turns sharing their sweetest memories of the past year and their hopes for the upcoming year.

The tenth day of the Jewish calendar is called Yom Kippur, or the Day of Atonement. In contrast to Rosh Hashanah, Yom Kippur is a much more solemn holiday devoted to prayer and repentance. Some spend the

Within this house, may there be no sorrow.
Within this house, may there be no distress.
Within this house, may there be no cruelty.
Within this house, may there be no strife.
Within this house, may there be blessings and peace.
—Traditional, Hebrew

Great is the glory of our name for you, God.
Feed the world, bringing goodness to all,
Preparing food for all your creations.
Blessed are You, who feeds the world.
—From the Birkat ha-Mazon (Blessing After the Meal)

The morning wind spreads its fresh smell.
We must get up and take that in,
That wind that lets us live.
Breathe, before it's gone.
—Rumi

May we draw strength
From the intricate dance of falling leaves,
The misty lavender skies,
The fields of ripened grain,
The silhouettes of wings flying south,
The abundant fruits of the earth—
Illuminated in all their glory
By the vibrant light of the harvest moon.
—Taz Tagore

entire day, beginning at sunrise on the eve of Yom Kippur and continuing for twenty-five hours, engaged in prayer. Others visit a *Mikva*, meaning "bath," to submerge themselves in water, a symbol of rebirth and renewal. Jenny, a Reformed Jew who lives in New York City, interprets Yom Kippur as a day of "at-one-ment." In some years, she dresses in white and attends prayer services at a local synagogue; in other years, she spends the day alone, hiking outdoors and reflecting on her life.

Sometimes in cooler climates, the weather stays balmy throughout September, a phenomenon called an "Indian summer." In most years, though, the wind acquires a brisk and blustery edge this month. September winds cause backyard trees to sway back and forth, and dry leaves to be tugged from branches. Swirling eddies in partially enclosed passageways, stairwells, and street corners lift leaves and pine needles in slow, mesmerizing spirals. Imbued with the scent of the apple harvest and distant rain, the autumn winds are a portent of winter.

The end of September is usually accompanied by the harvest moon—the full moon nearest to the autumnal equinox. It is so named because it enabled farmers to harvest well into the night, guided only by the light of the moon. The perfectly round, pale yellow, radiant harvest moon is the perfect icon for September—a reminder of the month's perfect temperatures, ripe harvest, and the search for intellectual enlightenment. Many autumn prayers and blessings pay homage to the harvest moon.

OCTOBER: *Making Quiet Discoveries*

The calls of wild geese—growing louder and more determined each day—are a sure sign that autumn has arrived. Like migrating birds, we too begin to prepare for winter in October. This is the month when we wrap ourselves in soft shawls and scarves before setting foot outdoors. It is a time to marvel at the spectacular display of fall colors on a warm afternoon. However, the waning temperature in October beckons us to turn our attention inside and to prepare our homes and ourselves for the winter.

By October, autumn colors have taken hold of the landscape—the natural world is a composite of ochre, burgundy, cadmium, and bronze. The leaves delicately twirl and float on their evitable dance toward the earth. Electric-red maple leaves are perfect for pressing between the pages of a dictionary or inserting in autumn party invitations. Huge piles of leaves accumulate in forests, parks, and backyards, beckoning us to jump in. The smell of bonfires and burning leaves wafts through the air. The colorful leaves are nature's final gift before winter.

In October our metabolism begins to shift in preparation for the winter season. The cold weather requires

The Great Spirit is in all things, is in the air we breathe.
The Great Spirit is our Father, but the Earth is our Mother.
She nourishes us; that which we put into the ground,
She returns to us.
—Big Thunder, Nineteenth-century Algonquin

us to sport warm sweaters and socks before stepping outside. This is the month when we perceptibly move, think, and speak a little bit more slowly. For many, October mornings involve repeated encounters with the snooze button, extending one's stay in bed. At work, people seem to linger in the lunchroom instead of returning to their desks. At home, cups of steaming tea and coffee prolong our communion at the dinner table. Much like the natural world, human beings adopt a slower and more deliberate pace in the month of October.

In addition to enjoying nature's colors outdoors, we prepare beautiful autumn ornaments for our homes in October. Early in the month, colorful wreaths and baskets appear in homes, schools, and offices. Inside classrooms, children create fall collages with pressed leaves, dried corn, and grains. The stunning variety of squash and corn at local markets and roadside farm stands are perfect for autumn centerpieces. Clusters of ornamental corn—especially the golden, Indian, raspberry, and squaw varieties—are lovely additions to a fireplace or porch. Wreaths hanging on front doors are vivid reminders of the upcoming fall harvest. By the end of the month, menacing jack-o'-lanterns, faux graveyards, and cobwebs—to ward off Halloween ghosts and goblins—become the focal point of our front yards.

On October 2, people from around the world celebrate **Gandhi Jayanti,** or Gandhi's birthday. Mohandas Karamchand Gandhi was born on October 2, 1869, in Porbandar, India. He became one of the most respected spiritual and political leaders of the modern world. Gandhi led the nonviolent resistance to free India from British rule. Gandhi stirred the spirits of the Indian people and awakened their pride and dignity. He was named the father of an independent India and given the name Mahatma, meaning "Great Soul." Gandhi also inspired future generations of activists, including the Civil Rights leader Martin Luther King, Jr.

On Gandhi Jayanti, readings from sacred texts such as the Upanishads and speeches written by Gandhi are recited at public holiday celebrations. The Thakrars, who live in England and India, are great admirers of Gandhi's philosophy and work. On his birthday, they select readings for the evening meal that awaken and celebrate the "mahatma" that resides within us all.

With the arrival of **Columbus Day** in mid-October—celebrated in North and South America, Italy, and Spain—people remember the famous explorer who set out to prove that the world was not flat. Christopher

Let us know peace.
For as long as the moon shall rise,
For as long as the rivers shall flow,
For as long as the sun shall shine,
For as long as the grass shall grow,
Let us know peace.
—Traditional, Cheyenne

Columbus, a brave Italian adventurer, convinced Queen Isabella of Spain that he would find a direct spice route to Asia if he sailed due west. On August 3, 1492, Columbus and ninety men set sail on the flagship *Santa Maria* accompanied by two other ships, the *Nina* and the *Pinta*. Two long months passed without any major discoveries. Then, on October 11, Columbus saw a light that was in fact, land. The next morning they arrived in America.

On October 12, 1866, the Italian population of New York City organized a celebration of the discovery of America; in 1905, Colorado became the first state to observe Columbus Day. President Franklin Roosevelt proclaimed October 12 to be Columbus Day in 1937—since 1971, it has been celebrated on the second Monday in October.

Many researchers credit the discovery of America by Europeans to early Scandinavian vikings or Irish missionaries who predated Columbus. And it is widely accepted that Native Americans settled the land several thousand years before. Even so, Columbus Day is a national holiday on which to contemplate, or question, the discovery of America. The Mielczareks, a lively Spanish family filled with artists and storytellers, have a special Columbus Day ritual. They select poems, stories, and films about great explorers and spend the holiday enjoying epic tales of daring and adventure. Even their favorite mealtime blessing, adapted from the writing of Joseph Campbell, speaks of heroism!

We have not even to risk the adventure alone,
for the heroes of all time have gone before us.
And where we had thought to find an abomination,
May we find a god.
Where we had thought to travel outward,
May we come to the center of our own existence.
And where we had thought to be alone,
May we be with all the world.
—Joseph Campbell (adapted)

He is the One Luminous, Creator of All, Mahatma,
Always in the hearts of the people enshrined,
Revealed through Love, Intuition, and Thought,
Whoever knows Him, Immortal becomes.
—The Upanishads

Strength does not come from physical capacity.
It comes from an indomitable will.
A person who has realized the principle of nonviolence
has the God-given strength for his weapon,
and the world has not yet known
anything that can match it.
—Mahatma Gandhi

Diwali, or the "Festival of Lights," is a floating holiday celebrated in October or November to mark the beginning of the Hindu New Year. The holiday's central figure is Lakshmi, the goddess of wealth and prosperity. On the first day of Diwali, Indians clean their homes, wash the steps leading to the front door, and decorate the path with colorful chalk designs. At dusk, thousands of tiny lamps adorning homes, buildings, and streets are lit. Stalls and markets, serving sweets and spicy snacks, line the major thoroughfares of every Indian village during Diwali. Throughout the holiday, evenings are spent at the local temple and visiting family and friends to exchange good wishes and plates of food. The New Year festival affects homes, schools, *and* offices—Indian businesses usually begin the new fiscal year on the fifth day of Diwali.

This ritual is One.
The food is One.
We who offer the food are One.
The fire of hunger is also One.
All action is One.
We who understand this are One.
—Traditional, Hindu

For Indians living abroad, the spirit of Diwali is awakened by lighting *dayas* (baked clay lamps filled with coconut oil) and preparing *malas* (flower wreaths). Dressed in their finest clothing and jewelry, Indian families visit temples to pray to Lakshmi and to make offerings of fruits, flowers, and sweets. Hindu blessings are recited at temple and before meals to pray for prosperity, health, and oneness with God in the New Year. Afterward, people visit the homes of friends and relatives to

Autumn
and our hearts
are seeking grace.
All around us
nature bids us
change.
Accept and give thanks
for falling
into surrender.
Into trust
that we will be held
and our brokenness
made whole.
— bell hooks

eat and to exchange gifts. Diwali parties are known to last until dawn—after a late dinner and a colorful fireworks display, people dance and sing to Bollywood favorites.

October nights bring light frost that tinges outdoor herb gardens and plants. October is the month in which to move plants, window boxes, and flowerpots into sheltered spaces. Overhead, the last calls of hawks and geese ring through the sky. Birds and animals staying put for the winter season scurry around in search of forgotten berries and seeds. Farmers and migrant workers also work long days and nights in order to collect and store the last fruits of the harvest— apples, corn, carrots, potatoes, and beets. After a long, cold day in the fields, they eat and sleep for only a few hours before waking up at dawn to work until the last fruits have been brought in.

In October, bushels of apples materialize in supermarkets and roadside stands. The musky sweet perfume of the apple harvest is irresistible to passersby. McIntosh, Spy, Fuji, and Cortland apples serve as the perfect afternoon snack or to fill a freshly baked pie. Apples need never be wasted—leftovers can be pressed into apple cider, added to winter soups, or dried into tasty snacks.

In the colder climes of Canada, the autumn harvest is celebrated in the middle of October. Although the tradition began in 1879, the Canadian Thanksgiving holiday became official in 1957. On the second Monday of October, tables are piled high with plates of steaming food—delicately carved roast turkey and goose, mashed gold and sweet potatoes, roasted squash, and freshly baked pies. Afterward, a bonfire is lit—outdoors or

Oh, the Lord's been good to me.
And so I thank the Lord
For giving me the things I need:
The sun, the rain and the appleseed;
Oh, the Lord's been good to me.
—Johnny Appleseed Blessing

For the hay and the corn and the wheat that is reaped,
For the labor well done, and the barns that are heaped,
For the sun and the dew and the sweet honeycomb,
For the rose and the song, and the harvest brought home.
—From a Traditional Hymn, England

in the fireplace—to set the mood for storytelling and sing-alongs. Indulging in an extra helping of cold turkey or pie after hours of merry-making is a sure sign of a festive Thanksgiving holiday.

On the other side of the world, Ghana's **Odiwera**, or Yam Festival, begins in September and marks the beginning of a new year. Farmers march alongside villagers for a local parade. Afterward, the yams are chopped, mashed, and stirred into stews and puddings. Before the feast, beautiful prayers are chanted and sung, praising the gods for providing a sizeable harvest. The music and song continue throughout the night.

Hail, hail, hail.
May happiness come.
May meat come,
May corn come,
Just as the farmers work,
And look forward to the reaping,
So may we sit again as we are sitting now.
—Prayer of the New Year Festival, Ga of Ghana

The changing climate in October encourages communion around sport—in a stadium, a local park, or in front of the television. Football games—pitting our alma mater or professional league favorite against a formidable opponent—spark elaborate tailgate parties. In October, the World Series eclipses all else; everyone seems to be trading player statistics, recounting exciting moments from past games, and enthusiastically cheering their American or National League favorites. For many, nothing can beat partaking in a fifty-thousand-person wave after a baseball gets knocked out of the park.

Since the time of the ancient Hebrews, Jews have celebrated a harvest festival called **Sukkoth**, or the Feast of Tabernacles—an eight-day festival that begins on the fifteenth day of the Hebrew month of Tishri. The festival marks the forty years of wandering that preceded the Hebrew peoples' entry into the Promised Land—a time when food was scarce and a successful harvest meant the difference between life and death. Their temporary huts were called *sukkah*, or "tabernacles," hence the name of the festival.

During the Feast of Tabernacles, observant Jews build three-walled *sukkah* out of branches, leaves, gourds, and berries fashioned so that everyone can view the nighttime sky and stars through the roof. Historically, Jews were supposed to inhabit a *sukkah* for a period of seven days and perform all normal household rituals—including eating and sleeping—inside. The ritual was intended to test their personal strength by exposing them to the elements; it taught people of all backgrounds, both rich and poor, to live without luxury or physical protection. Today, most Jews use *sukkah* for family meals but sleep inside their homes. The

A circle of friends is a blessed thing.
Sweet is the breaking of bread with friends.
For the honor of their presence at our board
We are deeply grateful, Lord.
—Nineteenth-century blessing

Blessed are you, G-d, our Lord, king of the world,
Who brings forth bread from the ground.
—Hebrew Blessing over Bread

celebration of Sukkoth is joyous, and its symbols remind celebrants of the successful harvest season. After dinner, many families join together in song. The repertoire usually includes everything from old Yiddish folk songs to AC/DC!

The pagan festival **Samhain** begins after sunset on October 31. In Celtic tradition, this day marks the arrival of the New Year and a time to reflect upon the year passed. During Samhain, Celtic farmers brought their herds back from upland fields and moved them into the warmer lowland pastures and cattle sheds. Old and surplus stock were slaughtered

As this Season of Plenty begins,
We give thanks to the God and Goddess
For the food with which we are blessed.
As darkness follows light,
So lightness follows dark,
In perfect balance and in all things
This is the way of the mighty Gods,
Blessed be.
—Pagan Blessing

And so it is, we gather again,
The feast of our dead to begin.
Our Ancestors we invite, Come!
And follow the setting of the sun.
Welcome within the dead who are kin,
Feast here with us and rest here within.
Our hearth is your hearth and welcome to thee;
Old tales to tell and new visions to see!
—All Hallows' Eve Blessing

and the meat salted or smoked for the winter season. In the pagan tradition, October is also the month to shift one's focus from the physical to the spiritual realm. After harvesting the fields, everyone was encouraged to spend the dark season of the year in personal reflection and prayer.

Halloween is a holiday that invites playful mischief. Originally a Celtic harvest festival to honor the Lord of the Dead, the festival became known as All Hallows' Eve after the ninth century. According to Celtic lore, All Hallows' Eve was a spiritually sensitive time when the gates separating the living and the dead were opened. On this night, souls of loved ones returned home for a warm meal and prayers before returning to their graves. In some villages, people set communal bonfires to help illuminate the path home or, alternatively, to scare away unwanted spirits. Contemporary Halloween celebrations, involving scary masks, jack-o'-lanterns, witches, ghosts, and nighttime prowling, all evoke the spirit of the first All Hallows' Eve.

In the 1840s, Irish emigrants brought the holiday to North America, and it has since spread to many other nations. Now, Halloweenesque holidays are celebrated in Great Britain (Punkie Night), Canada, Ireland, America, Japan, and the Philippines! The Japanese celebrate Obon, a night equivalent to Halloween (but occurring in July), when spirits of the deceased are welcomed home with paper lanterns hung by garden gates. In the Philippines, Halloween is celebrated on October 31 by collecting money for the poor by day and telling ghost stories by night.

One of the most popular Halloween traditions involves carving a scary face into a hollowed-out pumpkin and lighting a candle inside. On Halloween night, jack-o'-lanterns signal one's readiness to reward those sporting costumes and shouting "trick or treat" with candy. Another popular Halloween activity is bobbing for apples, an outgrowth of the late-season apple harvest and the desire to create Halloween activities for children. Some families turn their basements into haunted houses and invite blindfolded children to place their hands inside bowls of faux human remains such as intestines (cold spaghetti), eyeballs (peeled grapes), and fallen teeth (corn niblets). Late Halloween nights are often spent sorting candy into piles (to keep and to trade), eating candy apples, chocolate bars, and lollipops, and watching scary movies or *Addams Family* reruns.

October—a month of transition—is filled with change. As the fields dry up, the birds fly south, and the leaves fall to the ground, nature prepares for a period of hibernation. In October, we shift our patterns too: we eat bigger, heartier meals, bundle up in warm clothing, and replace summer linens with flannel sheets and goose-down duvets. As the clock strikes midnight on All Hallows' Eve, a melted heap of wax inside the jack-o'-lantern signals the end of the month. Ready or not, the winter season is coming....

NOVEMBER: *Harvesting for the Winter*

The month of November is inextricably linked to the words "thank you." Although the magic words are spoken throughout the year, November holidays such as autumn harvest festivals and Thanksgiving invite us to pause and reflect upon our individual and collective blessings. In November, we gather together to stay warm and to spread the holiday spirit. By the end of the month, the holiday spirit has begun to take root inside our hearts. So, we shift our attention to readying ourselves to celebrate the final weeks of the calendar year.

In November, bare tree branches form dark silhouettes against the muted sky. The brightly colored foliage of October is now decomposing, helped by millions of earthly microbes that are willing and able to brave the cold weather. Eventually, they will release nutrients back into the earth and supply the raw materials for leaves and flowers to blossom in

> *May the love that is in my heart*
> *pass from my hand to yours.*
> —Traditional, American

> *May the air carry your spirit gently,*
> *May the fire release your soul.*
> *May the water wash you clean of pain and sorrow.*
> *May the Earth receive you.*
> *May the wheel turn again and bring you to rebirth.*
> —Starhawk

the spring season. Inside greenhouses and nurseries, poinsettias are carefully pruned and watered in preparation for the Christmas season. On the outskirts of town, tree farmers prepare freshly cut pine trees for the long drive into the city.

During the day, warm winter coats, fuzzy hats, and long scarves protect us from the icy November winds. Despite the increasingly cold weather, the first snowstorm of the year brings tremendous excitement. For Helena, a native Torontonian and winter sports enthusiast, the first snowfall of the year is a time to bundle up and chase snowflakes. With or without snow, chilly November nights demand warm pajamas, flannel bedsheets, and down-filled duvets. Insulated from the outside world under warm blankets, November nights invite us to dream fantastic, snowy dreams before morning comes.

On November 1, Christians celebrate **All Saints' Day** to honor saints and unknown martyrs, especially those without a dedicated holy day. The first All Saints' Day occurred on May 13, 609, when Pope Boniface IV accepted the Pantheon in Rome as a gift from the Emperor Phocas. He dedicated it to honor the Virgin Mary and all martyrs. During the reign of Pope Gregory III, the festival was expanded to include all saints, and a chapel at the basilica of St. Peter was dedicated accordingly. It is celebrated with special masses and prayers to honor the dead.

All Souls' Day is a Roman Catholic day of remembrance for friends and loved ones who have passed away. It is thought to follow All Saints' Day in order to shift the focus from those in heaven to those in purgatory. Many believe the holiday replaced the ancient pagan Festival of the Dead, when departed souls would return for a meal. Families set another place at the table and put candles in the window to guide the souls back home. On All Souls' Day, the Torres family, who hail from Cuba and are devout Catholics, attend morning church service and then visit the local cemetery to sprinkle holy water and fresh flowers on the graves of the ancestors.

As a prayer that is known and loved by many, the Lord's Prayer is often recited before the evening meal on All Saints' and All Souls' Days. It was composed for the apostles who asked Jesus Christ how to pray. In the latter part of the fourth century, it became an official part of Roman Catholic Mass.

Our Father, who art in heaven,
Hallowed be thy Name.
Thy kingdom come.
Thy will be done,
On earth as it is in heaven.
Give us this day our daily bread.
And forgive us our trespasses,
As we forgive those who trespass against us.
And lead us not into temptation,
But deliver us from evil.
For thine is the kingdom,
and the power, and the glory,
for ever and ever. Amen.
—The Lord's Prayer

Make us worthy, Lord,
To serve our fellow humans throughout the world,
Who live and die in poverty or hunger.
Give them through our hands,
This day their daily bread,
And by our understanding love,
Give peace and joy.
—Mother Teresa

For food that stays our hunger,
For rest that brings us ease,
For homes where memories linger,
We give our thanks for these.
—Traditional, English

Later, Pope St. Gregory invited Christians to recite the prayer before the breaking of the bread. It has been recited as a blessing before meals ever since.

Similar holidays are celebrated in Mexico: the first two days of November are called **Dias de los Muertos**, meaning Days of the Dead. Their observance combines the solemn element of honoring dead relatives with the playful side of Halloween. Mexicans put on feasts, picnics, and plays with members of their family and local community. Home altars are populated with baked-bread figures of dead men and women (also called "dead bread"), skeletons made of sugar, and tombstones crafted out of marzipan. Mexicans also clean the graves of loved ones and decorate them with brightly colored flowers.

The British celebrate a unique day of thanksgiving in November called **Guy Fawkes Day**, or Bonfire Night. The holiday, celebrated on November 5, commemorates the discovery of a 1605 plot to kill King James I and blow up the Houses of Parliament. When Guy Fawkes was seized and the British throne saved, Parliament decreed a national day of thanksgiving. According to tradition, Brits create an effigy of Guy Fawkes and then burn it in a bonfire. Some children even keep up the tradition of carrying the effigy called "the Guy" through the streets and begging passersby for "a penny for the Guy." Monies collected are typically spent buying fireworks for the evening's festivities. Later that night, the Guy is placed atop a bonfire and everything is set ablaze. As the flames rise from the ground, colorful fireworks burst into the sky.

On Guy Fawkes Day, many recite a special prayer of thanksgiving before the evening meal. Afterwards, people gather in town squares and parks to celebrate among their friends and neighbors. Lewes, in the Southeast of England, is famous for its Bonfire Night festivities and attracts thousands of visitors each year. Bonfire Night is not only celebrated in

Britain—the tradition crossed the ocean and is celebrated in some parts of New England, New Zealand, and Newfoundland.

In Canada, England, France, and the United States, November 11 is a special day. On this day, called Armistice, Veterans, or **Remembrance Day**, people engage in a moment of silence to commemorate the end of World War I. On the eleventh hour of the eleventh day of the eleventh month of the year, the original armistice was signed, marking the end of the war and enabling soldiers to return home. During the moment of silence held at 11:11 A.M., we remember the soldiers who fought on our behalf. Groups of veterans and their families organize special services and gatherings to commemorate the loss of loved ones and read excerpts from poems such as "In Flanders Fields," by John McCrae. North Americans wear red poppies on their lapel, evoking the poppy fields surrounding the graves of lost soldiers.

Many countries with an agricultural tradition celebrate a seeming miracle in November—the autumn harvest. Harvest ceremonies—the precursors of our modern festivals—sprung up as our ancestors observed the endless cycle of birth and death around them. Since crops grow out of the earth and dead bodies are buried underground, people believed that crops contained human spirits. Fear of these spirits—commonly known as

In Flanders Fields the poppies blow
Between the crosses, row on row
That mark our place; and in the sky
The larks, still bravely singing, fly
Scarce heard amid the guns below.

We are the Dead. Short days ago
We lived, felt dawn, saw sunset glow,
Loved and were loved, and now we lie
In Flanders Fields.
—From "In Flanders Fields," John McCrae

Praise be to the Lord of the Universe
Who has created us and made us into tribes and nations
That we may know each other,
Not that we may despise each other. . . .
Most gracious are those who walk on the Earth in humility,
And when we address them, we say, "Peace."
—Muslim Prayer

We thank Thee, then, O Father,
For all things bright and good,
The seedtime and the harvest,
Our life, our health, our food.
Accept the gifts we offer,
For all Thy love imparts,
And, what Thou most desirest,
Our humble, thankful hearts.
—Matthias Claudius

corn spirits —lasted until the Middle Ages and inspired harvest charms, incantations, and rituals. Farmers prayed before removing crops from the earth, to avoid angering spirits who might seek revenge.

The ancient Greeks declared a day of Thanksgiving to honor Demeter, goddess of agriculture, with a day of prayer and feasting. The Romans honored Ceres, goddess of corn, during **Cerelia**, the Roman harvest festival. Fearing their good fortunes would not be repeated, the Romans always offered the first fruits of the harvest to Ceres. Afterwards, the Romans celebrated in grand style. The festivities began with people parading through the fields, playing music and singing. Later, they feasted, and then gathered in public spaces for theater, music, and dance. In the spirit of the Romans, the festival often lasted for days, or even weeks!

During the nineteenth century, some English farmers practiced charms and other rituals to ensure a good harvest for the coming year. They complemented their individual prayers with a community harvest festival called **Harvest Home**. The festival began after the last of the corn was cut; a small offering of corn was then piled into a cart and decorated with green branches, flowers, and ribbons. Some villages selected a

Without Thy sunshine and Thy rain,
We could not have the golden grain.
Without Thy love we'd not be fed;
We thank Thee for our daily bread.
—Traditional, Christian

lord and lady of the harvest—a couple who rode in the cart as it toured the fields. As the cart was drawn, fieldworkers walked alongside, cheering, laughing, and ringing bells. Others hid in the bushes along the path and threw buckets of water—a good-luck charm to bring rain—as it passed. The lord and lady of the harvest were usually drenched with water by the time the cart reached the decorated barn at the end of the tour. After a healthy feast, the harvesters played games, danced, and sang.

Although eight countries observe an official **Thanksgiving Day**—Argentina, Brazil, Canada, Japan, Korea, Liberia, Switzerland, and the United States—America has embraced its national day of thanksgiving with special delight. American Thanksgiving has evolved from a regional Puritan holiday to a nationwide celebration embraced by people of all faiths. The holiday honors the 1621 harvest—the year after the Pilgrims landed in America, sowed their fields, and prayed for enough food to survive the harsh winter. A Native American named Tisquantum, or Squanto, taught the Pilgrims to build watertight, round-roofed houses, use medicinal plants for healing, and till the land. The following summer, after being blessed with plenty of rain and sunshine, the fields bore fruit. The crop consisted of beans, squash, and an enormous yield of corn. Thus the Pilgrims finally had cause to declare a day of thanksgiving. Breaking from Puritanical tradition, they celebrated with prayer and a plentiful feast. The food, games, prayer, and merrymaking that marked the first American Thanksgiving laid the foundation for centuries of holiday traditions.

Even after three hundred years, Thanksgiving has retained its core elements: family, feasting, prayer, and merrymaking. By the late seventeenth century, it was already an important family holiday. As families became more dispersed—owing to young people seeking work in larger cities—Thanksgiving was an ideal time for families to congregate, share news, and celebrate.

Harvest Home! Harvest Home!
We've plowed, we've sowed,
We've reaped, we've mowed,
We've brought home every load,
Bless us all, Harvest Home.
—Harvest Home Blessing

Lord of the mountains and valleys.
You are my mother and my father.
You give rain for corn to grow
and sunshine to ripen it.
Now with your strength, the harvest begins.
I offer you the first morsels of the harvest.
My gift to you is only a small token
Of the enduring love you have given to me.
—Sioux Harvest Prayer

The farther people were scattered, the more meaningful the homecoming. Today American workplaces are closed on Thanksgiving Day and often on the following Friday, enabling people to enjoy a four-day weekend. This usually translates into one of the busiest travel days as people crisscross the country to celebrate with their immediate and extended families. Regardless of whether we are sleeping in a bed, on the sofa, or

Peace be unto thee, stranger, enter and be not afraid . . .

I have swept the hearth and lighted the fire . . .

The table is laid and the fruits of Life are spread before thee.

The wine is here also, it sparkles in the light . . .

Sit and rest and refresh your soul.

Eat of the fruit and drink the wine.

All, all is yours and you are welcome.

—From introduction to *The Science of Mind*, Ernest Holmes

on the floor, Thanksgiving is a time to reconnect with parents, siblings, extended family, and childhood friends. After months of phone conversations and e-mail messages, Thanksgiving weekend is a time to reconvene face-to-face to share stories and laugh with loved ones.

In an age of fast food and prepared meals, Thanksgiving stands out as a time when people go to great lengths to prepare a fresh, home-cooked meal. Mashed potatoes, baked or roasted squash, corn on the cob, and bean casseroles are popular Thanksgiving dishes. A longtime favorite is the peculiar (but delicious) combination of sweet potatoes and melted marshmallows! Fowl such as turkey, geese, ducks, and pheasants are traditional game meats associated with Thanksgiving meals. However, the turkey—a large and meaty bird suitable for feeding large groups of people—has been traced back to ancient Mayan harvest festivals and is the favorite centerpiece of the Thanksgiving table. Rich gravies and fruity sauces—made from cranberries or gooseberries—are generously poured on top of slices of warm turkey meat. Freshly baked pies filled with pumpkin, sweet potato, apples, or blueberries, are most commonly served after the meal. After nearly four hundred years, the traditional American Thanksgiving menu, including the way in which it is prepared and served, is essentially intact.

Since its inception, Thanksgiving has been both a social and religious holiday. Although the religious composition of America has shifted dramatically, most Americans continue to bow their heads and pray before carving the turkey. An early historical account of the Thanksgiving meal described the eldest member of the family rising and recounting the trials and triumphs of the year passed. The storytelling reminded everyone of how much they had to be thankful for; then, they bowed their heads and prayed.

Today, people of all faiths and backgrounds pray before the Thanksgiving meal. Some recite a blessing drawn from the Bible, Koran, Torah, or other sacred text. Others perform simple rituals in which everyone articulates—in silence or aloud—their feelings of gratitude. A wonderful Quaker blessing involves holding hands and engaging in a moment of silence. Afterwards, the eldest person initiates a hand squeeze; when it has passed through every hand at the table, the silence is broken and the meal begins. The Youngs, a very large interfaith family based in Chicago, developed a sweet Thanksgiving tradition that can be practiced by people of all faiths. They tuck M&M's inside each guest's dinner napkin. Before eating, each person counts the number of M&M's in their napkin and recites a blessing for each candy. In this way, saying grace creates a pleasant taste in their mouths and a fun-loving spirit at the table.

In a world where so many are hungry,
May we eat this food with humble hearts;
In a world where so many are lonely,
May we share this friendship with joyful hearts.
—Traditional, American

Parades and football games, hosted before and after the Thanksgiving meal, are a welcome distraction from the food. Ancient Egyptian harvest festivals featured great public parades in which the Pharaoh himself took part. Present-day parades are mounted along the main thoroughfares of American towns and cities. The annual Macy's Thanksgiving Day parade in New York City attracts hundreds of thousands of spectators and millions of television viewers. The elaborate floats, marching bands, and dancers make the parade a great joy to participate in or watch on Thanksgiving Day. Playing or watching football is another common American Thanksgiving tradition. After eating (or overeating), many families welcome the opportunity to get some fresh air and exercise on Thanksgiving Day. The Canner family, based in Cambridge, Massachusetts, mounts an exhausting football tournament on Thanksgiving that ends only when their fingers are too numb and cold to make another pass. Then they return home to invigorate their bodies with another helping of the Thanksgiving meal.

Rarely have any people enjoyed greater prosperity than we are now enjoying. For this we render heartfelt and solemn thanks to the Giver of Good; and we seek to praise Him—not by words only—but by deeds, by the way in which we do our duty to ourselves and to our fellow men.
—1902 Thanksgiving Day Address, President Theodore Roosevelt

Late November marks the beginning of the Christmas shopping season. While munching on leftover turkey, many compile their shopping lists and begin preparations for a winter holiday at home or abroad. Some take advantage of the cold weather (and accompanying rosy cheeks) by snapping family photographs for annual holiday cards. Others avoid holiday preparations altogether and spend the last few evenings in November sipping brandy and reading books by the fire. With the taste of Thanksgiving on the tips of our tongues and the holiday spirit growing in our hearts, the month of November draws to a close.

May we join hands around the dinner table,
To pray for the strength and patience to love one another.
May our circle grow with every birth and union,
Into a community united by love, rather than blood.
May every hardship make our circle stronger.
May it teach us that whenever we reach out in need,
Our hands will always be clasped in the palms of others.
—Taz Tagore

Christmas
Kwanzaa
Hanukkah
New Year's Eve
Chinese New Year
Martin Luther King, Jr., Day
Valentine's Day

Winter

DECEMBER: *Celebrating the Year*

December is a blessed month—in sound and in spirit. The sounds of December—hearty laughter, soothing song, and the enthusiastic clinking of glasses—echo our collective desire to make peace with and celebrate the passing year. The spirit of December is one of warmth and generosity: it is a time to count our blessings from the past year and to embrace the promise of a new beginning.

For the blessings you've bestowed upon this home and on this family,
For all the days we've had together and all the days to come,
For the joys and sorrows that bind us ever closer,
For the trials we've overcome,
And for teaching us that we can do no great things,
Only small things with great love.
We thank you.
—Traditional, American

Like the final grains of sand in an upturned hourglass, time seems to move more quickly in December. The days are a blur of work inside and outside the home—completing year-end projects, buying gifts, planning parties, coordinating travel plans, and baking goodies for friends and family. With only precious few weeks left in the year, December often delivers a second wind—a final burst of energy for tying together loose ends and celebrating the past year.

Much of nature's activity takes place behind closed doors: bears hibernate, hedgehogs burrow, and migratory birds take long vacations to southern climes. From time to time, it is possible to catch a glimpse of a shy deer, an indifferent rabbit, or a hungry field mouse. Usually, only their footprints are revealed in the white snow. Dried grasses and bare trees invite winter birds, such as chickadees and juncos, to take a rest after scavenging for lost seeds. In contrast, cardinals, so discreet during the summer mating season, now show their true colors. The flash of their red wings against a plain landscape mirrors the bright holiday colors inside our homes.

Despite the cold weather, December is a time to gather the troops, bundle up, and explore the great outdoors. What fun it is to career down a hill on a wooden toboggan or sail across the landscape on a pair of cross-country skis! Others prefer to carve perfect figure eights on a skating rink surrounded by a ring of snow-covered trees. When playing outdoors in December, every icy breath exemplifies the contrast between the wintry weather and our warm insides. After a long day of play, a mug of hot chocolate supplies enough warmth and energy for the long walk or ride home.

Twinkling lights hung from rooftops, window-panes, and branches electrify the dark December sky. Like a beacon, they illuminate the path ahead and sparkle with the promise of a new year. Stoking a fire over the December holidays gives us time to reflect upon the year. It is a time to view our low points with a newfound gentleness (and sense of humor) and to extend forgiveness to others and oneself. Doing so creates a warm glow on our faces and in our hearts.

December is a month in which to decorate our homes and offices with ornaments reflecting the holiday season. In early December, poin-settias appear in malls, flower shops, offices, and homes. Jews set out menorahs, dreidels, and ornaments depicting the Star of David. Christians hang stockings, Christmas ornaments, and colored lights.

Ah, fill the Cup:—what boots it to repeat
How Time is slipping underneath our Feet:
Unborn To-morrow, and dead Yesterday,
Why fret about them if To-day be sweet!
—The Rubáiyát of Omar Khayyám, Verse 37

Let us walk softly on the Earth
With all living beings great and small
Remembering as we go, that one God,
Kind and wise, created all.
—Traditional, American

Receive this holy fire . . .
May this light of God in you grow.
Light a fire that is worthy of your heads.
Light a fire that is worthy of your children.
Light a fire that is worthy of your fathers.
Light a fire that is worthy of your mothers.
Light a fire that is worthy of your God.

—Traditional, Masai

Kwanzaa celebrants fill their homes with traditional fabrics, sculptures, and candelabra that pay homage to their African ancestry. People of all backgrounds enjoy decorating their front doors with fresh boughs and wreaths decorated with winter berries. Some prefer edible ornaments such as chocolate-filled advent calendars with which to count down each day in December.

Even before the advent of the Gregorian calendar, human beings celebrated the conclusion of annual cycles in December. The **winter solstice** around December 21 commemorates the death of the old solar year and the birth of the new. It is also the shortest day of the year: from this moment on, the days will grow longer until the summer solstice. Newgrange, a beautiful circular stone structure in Ireland (believed to be several centuries older than Stonehenge and the pyramids), was built to receive a shaft of sunlight deep into its central chamber at dawn on the winter solstice.

Observing the movement of the sun on the winter solstice is much more dramatic in the northern regions of the world. In parts of Alaska and Canada's Northwest Territories, solstice ceremonies involve wearing animal skins—fox, bear, wolf—and offering thanks to all those who clothe and feed the community. Afterward, people eat, drink, and play games to test their stealth and endurance.

Pagans celebrate the winter solstice with fire—a symbol of the sun. The burning of a Yule log is a pagan tradition that is alive and well in Europe and North America today. Historically, the Yule log was the biggest log—the one most likely to burn for the whole night and into the New Year. As a symbol of the link between past and future, the Yule log was kindled with an unburned portion of the log from the previous year.

Even in ancient times people commemorated December by gorging themselves on meats, breads, pies, and winter vegetables. During the Roman festival **Saturnalia**, Saturn, the god of agriculture, was honored. Beginning prior to the solstice and continuing for a full month, Saturnalia was a time for feasting, games, and dancing. During this time, businesses, schools, and civic outposts were closed so that everyone could participate in the festivities. Animals that wouldn't survive the winter were slaughtered for the feasts. Wine that had been fermenting since the last grape harvest was ready to be drunk. Saturnalia was also a time when masters and slaves exchanged places. Masters waited on their servants, offering them choice cuts of meat, fine wines, and breads. In between feasts, Romans played pranks on each other or engaged in a mock trial in which Saturn was ritually sacrificed. Saturnalia relieved everyone's tensions by relaxing the rules and norms of Roman society for a whole month. Afterward, people returned to their daily routines feeling content and grateful.

As the Yule log is kindled,
So is the New Year begun,
As it has been down through the ages,
An unending cycle of birth, death and rebirth.
Every ending is a new beginning.
—Yule Log Blessing

When mirth reigns throughout the town and feasters about the house, . . .
When the tables beside them are laden with bread and meat,
And the wine-bearer draws sweet drink from the mixing-bowl and fills the cups;
This, I think in my heart, to be the most delightful of all to men.
—Homer

By the Middle Ages, Christianity had become the dominant religion in Europe. Just after the first millennium, Saturnalia evolved into a year-end Christian celebration called "Christes Maesse." Since Jesus's birth date is not known, Pope Julius I designated December 25 as **Christmas Day**—

God of harmony and peace,
Bless us as we enjoy the gifts
You have bestowed upon us.
May our eating together
Be a sign of the peace and goodness
You give to all people
Through your Son, Jesus Christ.
—Traditional, Christmas

a date that coincided with many long-standing pagan festivals and celebrations. The four-week Christian celebration of the Nativity is now a festive holiday across the globe.

Popular Christmas traditions involve caroling, decorating trees, and exchanging gifts. Caroling became immensely popular after the late eleventh century. Groups of carolers would travel from house to house, singing about the birth of Christ. As a reward for their efforts, they would be invited inside to share warm beverages and baked goods with the family. Caroling enabled neighbors to reacquaint themselves and to spread holiday cheer. Today, carols are sung for fun, communion, and spiritual expression. Some families even sing verses from their favorite Christmas carols—instead of a blessing—before the evening meal.

In 1616, Shakespeare's colleague Ben Jonson introduced a character called Father Christmas in one of his plays. Before long, the bearded Santa Claus, wearing white shoes and stockings and cloaked in a red furry gown, was promoting games, feasts, and the Christmas spirit. Not until 1822, when the American poet Clement Clarke Moore described Santa's elves, workshops, and reindeer, did his role and symbolism shift into a jolly, sleigh-riding bearer of gifts. Since then, Santa Claus has become a dominant figure in contemporary Christmas celebrations. Many leave out plates of cookies and glasses of milk to nourish Santa on his whirlwind tour of the globe on Christmas Eve. Some even write an advance note of thanks for the gifts that he will surely deliver.

Originally conceived by the Germans in the Middle Ages, the Christmas tree was adopted as an American tradition in the nineteenth century. As the new myths of Christmas merged, the

Let peace begin with me,
Let this be the moment now.
With every step I take,
Let this be my solemn vow.
—"Let There Be Peace on Earth"

Christmas tree became the center of gift exchanges. Every December, an enormous Norway spruce tree is installed, decorated, and lit at Rockefeller Center in New York City. The tradition began during the Depression, when workers building Rockefeller Center proudly placed a tree in the muddy construction site to lift their spirits. In 1933, a tree adorned with seven hundred lights was placed in front of the RCA building; in 1936, it was moved to the outdoor ice-skating rink at Rockefeller Plaza. In recent years, the Rockefeller Plaza tree has measured over seventy feet tall and has been outfitted with more than twenty-five thousand lights. Watching the Christmas tree lighting ceremony there has become a holiday tradition for many Americans.

Christmas celebrants can purchase a fresh evergreen tree from a local farmers' market, tree farm or winter fair. Lisa and Jimmy, a couple living in New York City, can't resist the

For reading my letter,
For traveling through the frosty night,
For delivering toys right to my doorstep,
And for doing it all with a wink and a smile,
I thank you, Santa Claus.
—Traditional Children's Blessing

oversize Christmas trees on sale in their neighborhood. Their gigantic tree is always the focal point of their annual holiday rituals and parties—because it nearly fills their modest living room! After decorating the tree, they host a bake-your-own-cookies party. Friends and family arrive with batches of their favorite cookie dough and spend the evening baking (and eating) cookies, singing carols, and admiring the tree. Their favorite carol, "O Christmas Tree," is the anthem for their party and the holiday season.

The shifting symbolism of Santa Claus and the Christmas tree are echoed in the way we create and exchange gifts. The first Christmas gifts were personal possessions that were offered as an act of friendship or love. With the advent of industrialism and the subsequent explosion of mass shopping culture, gifts evolved into items purchased at a store and exchanged with close family and friends. Rather than spending a lot of money, the Mitchell family spends a lot of *time* selecting considerate gifts.

For every year the Christmas tree,
Brings to us all both joy and glee.
O Christmas tree, O Christmas tree,
Much pleasure doth thou bring me!
—From "O Christmas Tree," German Christmas Carol

Based in Hamilton, Ontario, the Mitchells' holiday rituals are modest but thoughtful affairs. They often begin Christmas preparations in January and give themselves months to find the perfect tokens of their affection for each other. They recite this blessing (below) by Brother David Steindl-Rast before exchanging gifts on Christmas morning.

Others eschew traditional gift-giving and spend the holiday season offering time, money, and love to those in need. The Dadhiches, born into Hindu and Muslim families, spend the Christmas holidays volunteering at local shelters and soup kitchens. In addition to their time, they donate all the gifts they receive to people living in poverty. They also prepare special holiday baskets and drop them off at children's hospitals in the Toronto area.

The Matthews family begin their Christmas celebration on the morning of December 24 by stoking a fire, filling stockings, and stuffing the turkey. By the late afternoon, the meal is ready to be served and the priest of their parish recites a blessing for the entire family. The Christmas feast includes all the trimmings—roast turkey with stuffing, mashed potatoes, cranberry sauce, steamed vegetables, and roasted squash. After dinner, Mr. Matthews sits in a big, overstuffed chair and reads a hundred-year-old edition of *The Night Before Christmas* aloud. As night falls, everyone prepares to attend Midnight Mass. The interior of the church, lit only

In giving gifts, we give what we can spare,
But in giving thanks, we give ourselves.
One who says "Thank you" to another really says
"We belong together."
—Brother David Steindl-Rast, *Gratefulness, The Heart of Prayer*

by candles, evokes a solemn and holy mood among parishioners. Usually, one member of the Matthews clan sings a hymn during the service. The next morning, everyone gathers around the tree to open gifts, drink eggnog, tell stories, and celebrate the presence of immediate and extended family members. For the Matthews family, enacting age-old traditions is an important part of the holiday season.

The holiday season is filled with opportunities for honest and heartfelt expression. After filling (and refilling) glasses with holiday punch, many seize the opportunity to pay tribute to treasured colleagues, friends, and family members. Although the Irish didn't invent the practice of toasting, they certainly perfected the art form. Their witty, melodic, and warm-hearted invocations are often recited during the holiday season. In the Irish tradition, toasts are lighthearted expressions of appreciation.

Hanukkah, or the "Festival of Lights," is a Jewish holiday that begins on the twenty-fifth day of the Hebrew month of Kislev and continues for eight days. It can be traced back to the 165 B.C.E. desecration of a Jerusalem temple after local Jews refused to convert to Hellenism. Led by Judas Maccabeus, an army of Jewish rebels drove out the Syrian forces and recaptured the temple. During the temple's rededication, they fixed the broken menorah (a symbol for the light of God) but found enough oil for only one day. They lit the menorah, and miraculously the oil lasted a full eight days. Hanukkah is a festive holiday when Jewish families gather for eight consecutive nights to light the candles of the menorah. After sundown, a short blessing is recited and an additional candle is lit. The menorah is then displayed in a doorway or window until the candles burn out. In some parts of Jerusalem, families light the menorah, eat dinner, and then take a long walk through the neighborhood to admire the thousands of menorahs displayed throughout the town—a radiant reminder of their faith and community.

The Cohen family owns an antique menorah that has been passed down through many generations. After lighting the candles, they spend thirty minutes in quiet reflection, remembrance, or prayer. Then they

Always remember to forget
The troubles that passed away.
But never forget to remember
The blessings that come each day.
—Traditional Irish Toast

And (we thank You) for the miracles,
And for the salvation,
And for the mighty deeds,
And for the victories,
And for the battles,
Which You performed for our forefathers
in those days, at this time.
—Traditional, Jewish (recited on Hanukkah)

exchange small gifts with one another and share a festive meal. Every member of the Lorant family is given a menorah when they are big enough to light it. The menorah usually reflects their age and personality. As a child, Jenny Lorant had the smallest menorah and filled it with birthday cake–sized candles until she was old enough for a larger, adult version.

Kwanzaa, a holiday created by the African-American community in the 1960s, begins on December 26 and ends on New Year's Day. This holiday promotes celebration of one's family, God, and African ancestors. For seven consecutive nights, African-American families light a candle that represents one of seven principles underlying Kwanzaa: *Umoja* (Unity), *Kujichagulia* (Self-Determination), *Ujima* (Collective Work and Responsibility), *Ujamaa* (Cooperative Economics), *Nia* (Purpose), *Kuumba* (Creativity), and *Imani* (Faith). Lighting a candle is intended to evoke discussion or stories about the underlying meaning and significance of each principle. While each family celebrates Kwanzaa in its own way, nightly celebrations often

For the Motherland, cradle of civilization.
For the ancestors and their indomitable spirit.
For the elders, from whom we can learn much.
For our youth, who represent the promise of tomorrow.
For our people, the original people. . . .
For the Creator who provides all things great and small.
—From the Libation Statement, Kwanzaa

include a large traditional meal, storytelling, singing Christian and African songs, playing drums, and reading poetry.

The Greaves family celebrates Kwanzaa and Christmas together—in their view, the holiday season is a time to honor their African ancestry *and* their Christian faith. The holiday meals combine Southern specialties such as collard greens, coconut cake, and sweet potato pie with traditional American dishes such as roast turkey and mashed potatoes. Before the meal, they all join hands, bow their heads, and sing a song of praise.

In some years, the Greaveses sing a traditional spiritual—a combination of Protestant hymns and African music that was sanctioned by slave-owners. Some spirituals engaged the whole body—through foot stamping, hand clapping, and head-shaking—into a state of religious fervor. Frequently, spirituals were created spontaneously, with one singer improvising verses in between choruses repeated by the group. The flexible structure of the spirituals allowed the slaves to speak out on nearly every topic that affected their lives.

Count your many blessings,
Name them one by one;
Count your many blessings,
See what God has done.
—Traditional Gospel Song

The British created a unique holiday to honor the people on whom they depend throughout the year. On December 26, or Boxing Day, they offer small gifts of money to mail, milk, and newspaper deliverymen. The name of the holiday stems from the practice of distributing money saved in boxes throughout the year. Today, Boxing Day is celebrated in England, Australia, New Zealand, and Canada with sporting events (including the opening day of the circus) and special one-day sales for tardy gift-givers and enthusiastic shoppers.

To God be the glory, great things he had done!
So loved he the world that he gave us his Son,
Who yielded his life—an atonement for sin,
And opened the life gate that all may go in.
—Nineteenth Century Spiritual

Everywhere we go in December, the sounds of bells jingling, Christmas carols, and laughter follow closely behind. December is a month of merrymaking. Even the most serious or somber among us are prone to poke fun and have a good laugh in December. From the

May we be a protector to those without protection
A leader for those who journey
And a boat, a bridge, a passage,
For those desiring the other shore.
—Traditional, Buddhist

ancient Roman festivals to present-day holiday parties, December is a month in which to shrug off past misgivings and embrace those who challenged us throughout the year. December parties are known for copious servings of holiday punch and hors d'oeuvres followed by uninhibited dancing. For some, the merrymaking continues well after the party has ended. Some spread holiday cheer by toasting and serenading perfect strangers on their way home! December is a month in which to pop the cork on the year and allow our inner joy to bubble to the surface.

In preparation for New Year's Eve, people reflect on what to strive for in the coming year. Some resolve to break old habits such as smoking or eating poorly; others resolve to achieve lofty personal or professional goals. In response to years of broken resolutions, my friend Alison now sets positive aspirations for herself on New Year's Eve. She strives to spend more time with friends, achieve a better work-and-life balance, or to simply have more fun.

Go, eat your bread with joy,
And drink your wine with a merry heart.
—Ecclesiastes 9:7

Her approach has worked beautifully—for two consecutive years she kept her New Year's resolutions and had fun all the while!

The Hajim family, who hail from different parts of the country but gather together for the winter holidays, spend the afternoon of New Year's Eve reflecting on their aspirations for the New Year. In the early evening, they gather together to read their previous resolutions and to discuss what went "right" and what went "wrong." Individuals are applauded for sticking with a particularly thorny resolution and gently reprimanded for letting others slide. Next they share their resolutions for the coming year. Brad tries to balance his resolutions between those that will be easy to keep and those that will test his personal resolve. The family resolutions are recorded and then e-mailed out the next morning. In this way, the Hajims keep each other motivated (and accountable!) throughout the year.

And there's a hand, my trusty fiere,
And gie's a hand o' thine
And we'll tak a right gude-willie waught,
For auld lang syne.
—From "Auld Lang Syne," credited to Robert Burns

The excitement and fervor of December finally climax on **New Year's Eve** at the "witching hour." In Ecuador, New Year's Eve celebrations revolve around the *año viejo*, meaning "old year." The *año viejo* is a scarecrow made with old clothes and stuffed with sawdust and wood shavings. Most Ecuadoreans make the body at home and then purchase a papier-mâché head that resembles an old man. Before placing the head on top of the body, firecrackers are stuffed inside. At midnight, the *año viejos* are taken out into the street and set on fire. Amidst the leaping flames and fireworks, everyone bids farewell to the year passed.

In many English-speaking countries, people mount elaborate New Year's Eve parties in restaurants, bars, clubs, living rooms, and on rooftops. At the stroke of midnight, the moment that belongs equally to the past and the future, some sing "Auld Lang Syne," meaning "old long ago," or simply, "the good old days." In New York City, people count down the final moments of the year in Times Square and then embrace loved ones, friends, and passersby. The sound of cheers, noisemakers, and a final countdown are the delightful notes upon which December, and the calendar year, are brought to a close.

Grant me one more minute to taste the fruits of life,
Grant me one more hour to share them with others,
Grant me one more day to plant new seeds,
And thereby grant me a life that endures for eternity.
—Taz Tagore

JANUARY: *Anticipating the Future*

The month of January was named after the Roman god Janus, who was believed to have two faces: one looking back at the past and one looking forward to the future. Similarly, the month of January evokes the feeling of standing on a precipice between the year passed and the year to come. It is a time to set our sights on a magnificent year and then boldly set out to achieve it. In early January, we pause, reflect, and collect our strength. By the end of the month, we ready ourselves to courageously leap into the New Year.

The color of January skies alternates between vivid blue and powdery gray; the January sun often hides under a thick blanket of clouds and emanates only muted rays of light. January storms arrive without warning and bring crystalline snowflakes that cling to coats and eyelashes. The snow lingers long enough for children to build lopsided snow-people, toss icy snowballs, and trace snow angels on their way home from school. Long commutes home afford an opportunity to contemplate the vast horizon and the empty sky. Haiku is an ancient Japanese poetic tradition that celebrates the natural world. With only a few words, haiku masters like Hashin could express appreciation for even the starkest days of the year.

Few animals and birds are visible during the short days of January. On rare occasions, a brave flock of starlings might be spotted scavenging for remaining berries. In the trees, rivers, and pastures, nature is resting and preparing for rebirth. After a long month of lifelessness and silence, early signs of new life emerge. The buds of oak and maple trees enlarge under a blanket of snow, and the white flowers of hellebore tentatively blossom.

In the beginning was the Word,
And the Word was with God, and the Word was God.
The same was in the beginning with God.
All things were made by Him; and without Him
was not anything made that was made.
In Him was life; and the life was the light of men.
—John 1:1-4 (King James)

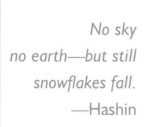

No sky
no earth—but still
snowflakes fall.
—Hashin

In some parts of the world, New Year's Day is celebrated with a special meal. The meal varies from region to region: the English favor roast ham or beef, Texans eat lucky black-eyed peas, Swedes prepare *lutfisk* and rice pudding, and some Native American tribes prefer roasted salmon and acorns. A hearty meal has the ability to make us feel courageous and whole; a New Year's Day feast can inspire a feeling of readiness for the upcoming year.

January invites quiet activities—reading books, handcrafting, and watching movies. It is the perfect month for starting an epic novel or biography that has been sitting on the bookshelf for years. It is a month in which to drift in and out of our reading, appreciating the unbroken time in which to savor contemporary or classic literature.

Knitting, stitching, and needlepointing are tranquil activities for a solitary afternoon in January. Knitting helps us keep our fingers moving and our mind off the cold weather. After establishing a slow, purposeful rhythm, balls of yarn and time quickly unravel. After several hours of tracing and retracing the same patterns, individual stitches form a beautiful whole. The resulting blanket, scarf, or sweater is perfect for warming up body and spirit. Some people knit prayer shawls to bring comfort to those facing a particularly difficult time in their lives or grieving the loss of a loved one. An age-old Jewish tradition, prayer shawls are blessed and then laid upon the shoulders of those in need as a reminder of God's grace and the loving hands of the knitter.

January is a good time to watch our favorite Hollywood movies from the past and present. Nestled on the sofa with a bowl of popcorn and a blanket, we accompany our favorite characters on wild adventures through time and space. Watching them move to a new place, fall in love, have children, and grieve inspires us to kick-start our own journeys into the year.

Throughout January, rich stews, soups, and casseroles populate our dinner tables. The first mouthful of warm, soft food tastes like heaven and helps thaw frozen fingers and toes. During cold winter months, dinner

Life is ending? God gives another.
Admit the finite. Praise the infinite.
Love is a spring. Submerge.
Every separate drop, a new life.
— Jalal al-Din Rumi

Everyday blessed
in every way blessed,
no need to ask,
divine spirit offers,
with open hearts,
with hands ready,
we receive.
—bell hooks

We pray tonight, O God,
for confidence in ourselves,
our powers and purposes
in this beginning of a New Year.
Ward us from all lack of faith and hesitancy
and inspire in us not only the determination
to do a year's work well,
but the unfaltering belief that
what we wish to do, we will do.
—W. E. B. Du Bois

May this food restore our strength,
Giving new energy to tired limbs,
New thoughts to weary minds.
May this drink restore our souls,
Giving new vision to dry spirits,
New warmth to cold hearts.
And once refreshed,
May we give new pleasure to You,
who gives us all.
—Traditional, American

plates are quickly emptied and everyone unabashedly asks for second helpings. The weather inspires us to linger at the dinner table a little longer than usual, until the mealtime chitchat diminishes into silence. Only then do we retire to the living room with a cup of steaming tea or hot chocolate to wait for our swollen bellies to subside.

In many parts of the world, a feeling of optimism permeates January's holidays and festivals. In Norway—a northern country where winters are marked by an absence of sunlight—people celebrate **Sun Day** in late January. With the reappearance of the sun, Norwegian schools and offices close for a few days so that everyone can participate in the festivities. In some villages, people take an icy dip in a local lake and then warm up in a hot sauna. Others celebrate with huge feasts featuring platters of pickled fish, caviar, brown cheese, and locally brewed beer. Often, an entire town will eat, drink, and dance until the early morning to honor the arrival of the January sun.

Both the Chinese and Iroquois peoples mount New Year's festivals after the first moon of the year. As floating holidays, they occur between early January and February. The Iroquois nation hosts eight-day celebrations in which people feast, dance, and perform sacred ceremonies in traditional dress in the month of January. On January 10, the Iroquois practice special rituals dedicated to the renewal of body and spirit. Tribe members dressed as curing spirits visit homes and longhouses in the local community. They greet and bless each member of the tribe to inspire good health and uplift people's spirits.

The Chinese astrological calendar follows a twelve-year lunar cycle, with each year named after a sacred animal. Observed for fifteen days after the first new moon, **Chinese New Year** celebrations involve several special traditions. Prior to the New Year, Chinese families thoroughly clean their homes to "sweep out" all the bad luck. Then they decorate windows and mantels with red wall hangings, lanterns, and ancient symbols. The first two days—New Year's Eve and New Year's Day—are celebrated with immediate family. Youngsters pay respect to parents and elders, lai see envelopes (filled with "good luck" money) are exchanged, and special meals are prepared. The Chao family spends New Year's Eve listening to great-aunts, great-uncles, and grandparents recount ancient Chinese myths related to the animal spirit of the year. The stories help set the tone for the year and inspire everyone to write three New Year's resolutions on slips of paper. After reading their resolutions aloud, everyone is applauded and toasted with tea, Chinese beer, and rice wine.

After the first two days, Chinese families visit extended family members, neighbors, and friends to spread good wishes for the coming year. Bearing plates of lucky foods such as Mandarin oranges, whole fish, and noodles, they spend hours in each other's living rooms eating and talking about the past year. Visits often spawn intense mahjong tournaments that can last for days or weeks. On the fifteenth day, there is a Lantern Festival—a parade featuring beautiful Chinese lanterns, dancing dragons, food, and music. The golden light of the lantern and the fearless Chinese dragons inspire visions of a lucky and prosperous year.

Three Kings Day is celebrated on January 6, twelve days after Christmas. Also known as the Feast of the Epiphany, or *Día de los Reyes* in Spanish-speaking countries, the Christian holiday commemorates the three kings who followed the star of Bethlehem to bring gifts to baby Jesus. According to the bible, kings—Melchior, Caspar, and Balthazar—presented Jesus with gold, frankincense, and myrrh. In Mexico and

Oh You who feed the little bird,
Bless our food, Oh Lord.
—Traditional, Norway

We return thanks to our mother the earth,
Which sustains us.
We return thanks to the rivers and streams,
Which supply us with water.
We return thanks to the sun, moon and stars,
Which give us their light.
We return thanks to the Great Spirit,
In Whom is embodied all goodness,
And Who directs all things for the good of Her children.
—Traditional, Iroquois

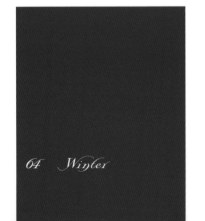

Round the table,
Peace and joy prevail.
May all who share this season's delight,
Enjoy countless more.
—Traditional, Chinese

Hail Mary, full of grace. The Lord is with thee.
Blessed art thou amongst women,
And blessed is the fruit of thy womb, Jesus.
Holy Mary, Mother of God, pray for us sinners,
Now and at the hour of our death. Amen.
—Traditional, Catholic

Puerto Rico, gifts are exchanged on Three Kings Day rather than on Christmas. In some parts of Central and South America, children fill their shoes with hay on the eve of the holiday. By morning, their shoes have been filled with toys and sweets. On this day, Mexicans also prepare *rosca de reyes*, a crown-shaped sweet bread decorated with pieces of orange and lime and filled with nuts, figs, and cherries.

Colleen, who has an American father and a Puerto Rican mother, remembers reciting Hail Marys on the morning of Three Kings. It was her way of offering thanks before playing with her new toys or indulging in holiday sweets. The prayer was recited as far back as the seventh century but it gained prominence as a blessing and salutation after the eleventh century. The prayer praises Mary's strength and resolve as the mother of Jesus.

In the United States, **Martin Luther King, Jr., Day** is celebrated on the third Monday in January. Dr. King, one of America's greatest civil rights leaders, was born on January 15, 1929. He helped ignite the Civil Rights movement in the 1950s and won the Nobel Peace Prize in 1963 for promoting nonviolent means to end racial segregation in America. His grand vision for social justice in America, his stewardship over thousands of peaceful protests, and his superb orations have inspired hope among people of all races and across the globe. On this day, Americans pay tribute to Dr. King's vision, accomplishments, and legacy.

For the Bowles family, Martin Luther King, Jr., Day is a time to rise early and study Dr. King's life and accomplishments. The family will visit an African-American museum, watch documentaries about black history, or discuss the leaders of the Civil Rights movement. Before the evening meal, they read an excerpt from one of Dr. King's sermons instead of reciting a traditional blessing. The speeches inspire appreciation for the freedoms they enjoy and motivate them to make their own unique contribution to society.

And when this happens,
when we allow freedom to ring . . .
we will be able to speed up that day
when all of God's children . . .
will be able to join hands
and sing in the words of the old Negro spiritual,
"Free at last! Free at last!
Thank God Almighty, we are free at last!"
—From "I Have a Dream" speech, Martin Luther King, Jr.

The end of January is a time in which to tackle New Year's resolutions with strengthened resolve. After all, resolutions are promises to write a new page in our book of life. They represent our desire to rise to new heights and to see ourselves in new and better ways. All it takes is one victory—politely declining a tantalizing brownie or waking up early enough for a morning workout—to feel invincible! January is the perfect time to quit smoking, join a gym, or take up a new hobby. In our race against time, January is a month to take positive steps in the direction of change.

May we equally embrace constancy
and the shifting sands of change.
May we revel in new beginnings
and remember the past;
Knowing that like two halves perfectly conjoined
every passing begets a twin: rebirth.
—*Taz Tagore*

FEBRUARY: *Savoring Love and Loved Ones*

For centuries, the month of February has been associated with love. February's holidays and festivals celebrate love of life, of one another, and of country. This month, we focus more time and attention on the heart. From this emotional epicenter, we appreciate those we love and who love us in return.

February skies yield snow, sleet, and eventually rain. The weather causes many people to experience the "February blues," a condition that we typically attribute to the cold weather and sunless sky. When the sun periodically bursts through the clouds, we turn our faces upward to meet the fleeting rays of sunshine. Some shake off the February blues by going to sleep early and waking up late. Others escape to warmer places such as Mexico, the Caribbean, or Southeast Asia and pass the time drinking margaritas and lying on the beach. Still others conquer the February blues by embarking on a final skiing, ice fishing, or snowmobiling adventure.

Brave winter birds venture out in February to scout new nesting areas and potential sources of food. As harbingers of spring, fragrant yellow flowers burst forth from textured branches of witch hazel. Dormant seeds stir in anticipation of their upcoming journey through the earth. In February, Mother Nature gently awakens from a lengthy slumber.

The food which we are about to eat
is Earth, Water and Sun,
Therefore, Earth, Water and Sun
will become part of us.
This food is also the fruit
of many beings and creatures.
We are grateful for it.
May it give us strength, health and joy—
and may it increase our love.
—Traditional, Unitarian

When we listen carefully to our restless hearts,
We may start to sense that
In the midst of our sadness, there is joy;
In the midst of our fears, there is peace;
And that indeed, in the midst of our irking loneliness,
We can find the beginnings of a quiet solitude.
—Henri J. M. Nouwen

Earth teach me suffering,
As old stones suffer with memory.
Earth teach me courage,
As the tree which stands alone.
Earth teach me freedom,
As the eagle which soars in the sky.
Earth teach me to forget myself,
As melted snow forgets its life.
Earth teach me regeneration,
As the seed which rises in the spring.
Earth teach me humility,
As blossoms are humble with beginning.
—Chief Yellow Lark, Lakota

Human beings have always heeded weather warnings from animals. An old *Farmer's Almanac* suggested that cows lie down before rainfall, coyotes howl louder if a storm is approaching, and swallows fly low to signal the onset of cold weather. So it is not unusual that we turn to a groundhog to pronounce the arrival of spring. On February 2, we celebrate **Groundhog Day**—the only holiday that is focused solely on weather conditions. Groundhog Day is celebrated at the midpoint between the winter solstice and the spring equinox—an inflection point between the seasons.

In its earliest incarnation, Groundhog Day was called Imbolc, a pagan fertility celebration. Imbolc is a Gaelic word, and on this day, people pray to Brigid, a Celtic fertility goddess. When the pagan holidays were transformed into Catholic equivalents, two new holidays emerged: Saint Brigid's Day, celebrated on February 1, and Candlemas Day, celebrated on the second day of February. On Imbolc, Celts placed a red ribbon on their doorstep to invite Brigid to bless their household. They also put out a bowl of buttered bread for the fairies that were believed to travel with Brigid.

On Candlemas Day, candles were lit to signify purification and, in some countries, to welcome increased daylight. In the Pyrenees, Candlemas was marked by a special bear ceremony—the emergence of a hibernating bear on February 2 was believed to accelerate the arrival of spring. Candlemas was eventually reincarnated as Groundhog Day, as indicated by the old Scottish couplet: "If Candlemas Day is bright and clear, there'll be two winters in the year." According to legend, if the weather is clear and the groundhog sees his shadow, there will be another six weeks of winter. By the 1840s the idea had caught on in the U.S., particularly in Pennsylvania, where the earliest European settlers were German immigrants. Today, Punxsutawney, Pennsylvania, with its furry mascot "Punxsutawney Phil," is the American headquarters for Groundhog Day celebrations. On the morning of February 2, Phil looks for his shadow at Gobbler's Knob, a wooded knoll just outside the town, and predicts when spring will arrive.

May Brigid bless the house in which you dwell;
Bless every fireside, every wall and door;
Bless every heart that beats beneath its roof;
Bless every hand that toils to bring it joy;
Bless every foot that walks its portals through;
May Brigid bless the house that shelters you.
—St. Brigid's Blessing

You are the everlasting source of light.
We stand before you,
Eyes shining and hearts open,
To receive the light of the season
And the warmth of your eternal love.
—Candlemas Blessing

In ancient Rome, February was considered the official start of spring and was filled with purification and fertility rituals. In fact, the word February comes from the Latin word *februa* meaning "feast of purification." During this month, Romans thoroughly swept their homes and sprinkled salt (for purification) and grains (for fertility) inside. Then they moved into the streets. **Lupercalia**, a festival celebrated on February 15, was a time of licentiousness and lovemaking. On this day, young Roman males slaughtered sacrificial goats. Donning goatskin loincloths, they struck young women across the palm with goatskin thongs to awaken their fertility. These ancient Roman festivals were the fertile ground from which Valentine's Day blossomed.

In third-century Rome, Emperor Claudius—believing that bachelors made better soldiers—forbade marriage. In defiance, a young priest named Valentinus secretly married couples by candlelight. Before he was caught and sentenced to death, throngs of young people visited him bearing notes that proclaimed the triumph of love over war. These notes are believed to be the first valentines. Later, the myth that Valentinus allegedly fell in love with the jailer's daughter and signed a love letter "Your Valentine" traveled across Europe. Valentinus was eventually named the patron saint of love and was prayed to during times of scarcity and need. Around the fourteenth century, he became inextricably linked to the only holiday dedicated to human love.

By the Middle Ages, February 14 had become a day for celebrating romantic love. In Elizabethan England, those besotted by love were instructed to express their feelings with small gifts. Romantic poetry, praising the beauty and temperament of one's lover, was composed and read aloud on Valentine's Day. It was also a holiday filled with mystical rituals: at midnight, young singles went to cemeteries to search for a love omen or placed hemp seeds in their beds to conjure dreams of a future lover.

In the 1840s, Esther Howland, the daughter of a stationer, developed a talent for creating hand-painted Valentine's Day cards. Her well-marketed cards, filled with sentimental messages and trimmed with lace, set off a trend. Many decades later, people began to send boxes of chocolate along with their cards. Chocolate contains phenylethylamine, or the "love molecule," a chemical that is released by the brain during sexual intercourse. As such, chocolate is said to be an aphrodisiac, a food that improves one's predisposition for love. The Japanese enjoy the Valentine's holiday so much that they created a second day (March 14) for men to receive love presents from admiring women!

May this water cast out all of my impurities
And transform me from lead to gold.
Purify my mind,
Purify my body,
Purify my heart.
It is so.
—Roman Prayer of Ablution

February 14 shifts our focus from the cold weather to the inner warmth of our hearts. The spirit of Saint Valentine reminds us that loving and being loved is what matters most. On this day, we celebrate our loved ones with special words, gestures and gifts that come from the heart. Matthew, an attentive husband who hails from Texas, takes his wife away on Valentine's Day and pampers her with massages and by reading love poetry to her. Helena and Ben, two newlyweds who

How do I love thee? Let me count the ways.
I love thee to the depth and breadth and height
My soul can reach, when feeling out of sight
For the ends of Being and ideal Grace.
—From Sonnet 43, *Sonnets from the Portuguese,* Elizabeth Barrett Browning

eloped and were married in Paris, buy a small collection of candles to place throughout their home and prepare a romantic holiday meal in the soft glow of candlelight.

February is also a month in which to commemorate the institution of marriage. The idea surfaced in 1981 when local couples encouraged city and state officials in Baton Rouge, Louisiana, to proclaim February 4 "We Believe in Marriage Day." By 1982, forty-three governors had officially proclaimed the holiday, and its observance spread to U.S. military bases. In 1983, the name was officially changed to World Marriage Day, and its theme—"Love One Another"—was established. It takes courage to love another person and to sustain a loving marriage, and in February, we celebrate both.

In February, many nations celebrate their country and countrymen with patriotic holidays. Americans celebrate Presidents Day on the third Monday in February to commemorate the birthdates of George Washington (February 22) and Abraham Lincoln (February 12). Washington set a stellar example of leadership as the first president of the United States. Though a capable military leader, Washington was most celebrated for his humility, determination, and strong moral compass—qualities that emanate from the heart. Similarly, Lincoln—the sixteenth president of the United States—guided America through the Civil War with enormous compassion and dignity. On January 1, 1863, he issued the Emancipation Proclamation, declaring all slaves free within the Confederacy. Throughout his tenure, Lincoln delivered eloquent speeches about balancing the role of government with the inalienable rights of the individual. National Freedom Day, celebrated on February 1, further reinforces the importance of Lincoln's presidency. On this day, Americans commemorate the 1865 signing of the Thirteenth

Sing and dance together and be joyous,
But let each one of you be alone.
Even as the strings of a lute are alone
though they quiver with the same music.
And stand together yet not too near together:
For the pillars of the temple stand apart,
And the oak tree and the cypress
grow not in each other's shadow.
—Khalil Gibran

One who knows distances
out to the outermost star
is astonished when he discovers
the magnificent space in your hearts.
—From "Antistrophes," Rainier Maria Rilke

Amendment to abolish slavery. Leaders such as Washington and Lincoln remind us of the legacy of compassionate political leadership in America. On this day, many read and draw inspiration from the writings of Lincoln and Washington. Their words remind us to appreciate rights and freedoms enjoyed in a democratic society.

Canada expresses national pride this month, too. On February 15, 1965, the country's red and white maple leaf flag was flown for the first time. In 1996, Jean Chrétien, then Prime Minister of Canada, declared February 15 to be **National Flag Day**. Although simple in design, the maple leaf flag represents the values of the Canadian people: freedom, peace, respect, and tolerance. Many Canadians traveling abroad affix a Canadian flag pin to their luggage to symbolize their national pride. Sometimes they offer these pins to others in a gesture of friendship.

On February 24, Mexicans celebrate their hard-won independence from Spain with **Día de la Bandera**, or Flag Day. On the week before the holiday, street vendors in Mexican cities sell flags of all sizes and shapes. The Mexican flag, created in 1821, has a central emblem referring to the Aztec legend that a city would be built wherever an eagle was seen devouring a serpent. The flag's colors—green, white, and red—symbolize hope, purity, and the blood of national heroes. Mexicans enjoy parades, speeches, and live music in the Plaza Central in Mexico City near the monument to General Vicente Guerrero, the

We offer thanks for the gift of togetherness.
May we honor our union
by forgiving our differences,
by opening our hearts to intimacy,
by strengthening our spoken and silent communication,
and by respecting the source of this and all love.
—Taz Tagore

We here highly resolve
that these dead shall not have died in vain—
that this nation, under God,
shall have a new birth of freedom—
and that government of the people,
by the people, for the people,
shall not perish from the earth.
——From The Gettysburg Address, Abraham Lincoln

Brothers and sisters,
Why do waves rise violently in the ocean?
Why do clouds hang darkly over mountain peaks?
Let us pray with all of our hearts
for peace and serenity
to inhabit the hearts of all beings
and every corner of the earth.
—Traditional, Mexican

first Mexican soldier to swear allegiance to the flag.

In many countries, February is a month for one last gasp of music, food, and alcohol before Lent. French explorers first celebrated Mardi Gras on the banks of the Mississippi River in 1699. On **Mardi Gras**, or "Fat Tuesday," the French feasted, sang, and danced in preparation for Ash Wednesday. The festival slowly spread to several Southern states and reached its zenith in Louisiana. In the French Quarter of New Orleans, residents and tourists take part in one of the most frenzied public parties in America. Mardi Gras revelers participate in the famous parade, catching beads, doubloons, cups, and trinkets that are tossed from colorful floats. In the evening, people flit from bar to bar drinking potent concoctions that are innocently topped with a ruby-red cherry or a tiny pink umbrella. Later in the evening, revelers dress up in elaborate costumes and attend masquerade balls, where they dance until the wee hours of the morning. For those who partake in a New Orleans–style Mardi Gras, a full week of vacation is required to recover!

Brazilian Carnival, another lavish festival before Lent, originates from the ancient Greek festival honoring Dionysus, god of wine. Its name comes from *carne vale*, or "farewell to the flesh." In 1840, Rio de Janeiro celebrated its first Carnival ball; a decade later it added a parade with horse-drawn floats and military bands. Today, Rio's lavish Carnival is world-famous: spectacular floats surrounded by thousands of dancers, singers, and drummers parade through Sambódromo stadium dressed in ornate costumes. Festivals like Carnival invite celebrants to indulge themselves with food, wine and dancing before beginning a period of restraint and purification in

Prepare us for tomorrow
By enabling us to taste the fullness
Of what we have today.
Tomorrow, we will experience some hunger.
May our fasting make us more alert
So that we are ready to hear your word
And respond to your call.
——Mardi Gras Blessing

March. Carnival prayers invite people to fast in order to remember and appreciate the joys of everyday life.

During the short month of February we begin to get relief from the long, dark winter nights. February, with its capacity for surprise, can last for an extra day. Every four years, the month is twenty-nine days long, owing to the asynchronous Gregorian and solar calendars. Just when you think it is over, February might deliver one extra day of winter. Leap Day is a good time to curl up on the sofa with a cup of hot cider and listen to the sounds of birds returning home and snow dripping from rooftops. These are the pleasant notes that herald the arrival of springtime.

Tomorrow we will fast,
Today, we feast.
We thank you for the abundance
That you have showered upon us.
As we partake in your wonderful gifts—
Food, song, and dance,
We commit ourselves
To share our bounty with others
For as long as we shall live.
—Carnival Blessing

May you grant us a sign—

a ray of sunshine…

the call of a bird returning home…

the unfolding of a delicate blossom…

a throb of life from above or below…

to mark the arrival of spring.

—Taz Tagore

Norouz
Lent
Saint Patrick's Day
Passover
Earth Day
Easter
Mother's Day

Spring

MARCH: *Purifying Hearts and Homes*

In March, the earth reaches an important point on its journey around the sun: the spring equinox. As the days gradually lengthen and the temperature rises, March throbs with a spirit of renewal. Surrounded by warm spring air, we celebrate the sun, new beginnings, and generosity towards others. This month we purify our hearts, homes, and gardens so that we can share the spring season with others.

Outside, the natural world is stirring. Just as we stretch our limbs after a long rest, nature sends delicate, yellow-green shoots out of the earth in search of sunlight. Dressed in furry jackets, the gray buds of the pussy willow are seasonal trailblazers; they valiantly brave the chilly weather in order to usher in the spring season. Once the earth thaws, crocuses break through the frosty soil and blossom in bright hues. Migrating robins return to rebuild nests for a new brood. At the end of March, the budding of birch trees is a sure sign that spring is on the way.

Now is the dark half of the year passing
Now do the days grow light,
And the Earth grows warm
I summon the spirit of these seeds
Which have slept in darkness
Awaken, stir and swell
Soon you will be planted in the Earth
To grow and bring forth new fruit.
Blessed be!
—Pagan Blessing

Around March 21, the sun rises exactly in the east, travels through the sky for twelve hours, and sets exactly in the west. There are only two days in the year when the sun carves a perfect arc through the sky: the spring (or vernal) and the autumnal equinoxes. The vernal equinox has been celebrated for thousands of years because it signaled an increase in food supply. Many ancient cultures built their greatest monuments—tombs, temples, cairns, and observatories—to align with the equinoxes. The Egyptians built the Sphinx so that it points directly toward the rising sun on the vernal equinox. Stonehenge is a perfect marker of the equinoxes and the solstices.

Bless us.

Bless our land and people.

Bless our forests with mahogany, wawa, and cacao.

Bless our fields with cassava and peanuts.

Bless the waters that flow through our land.

Be with us youth in our countries, and in all Africa, and in the whole world.

Prepare us for the service that we should render.

—Ashanti Prayer

The New Fire ceremony was an ancient Mayan ritual practiced on the spring equinox that reenacted the story of a humble god who hurled himself into the cosmic fire and thereafter birthed light and life. Afterward, Mayans symbolically started anew by throwing out their woven mats and breaking their dishware. In doing so, they sought to achieve harmony with the almighty sun.

The ancient Mayans also constructed hundreds of temples and observatories to mark the movements of the sun and stars. Chichen Itza, located on the northern part of the Yucatan peninsula, is the center of an important spring equinox celebration. Every year, tens of thousands of people travel long distances to watch the interplay of light and shadow on the stepped pyramid. By the late afternoon, seven half-diamond-shaped patches of light form a huge serpentine shadow; bystanders chant hymns, play drums, take pictures, pray, or simply watch in awe.

March is the month during which many nonprofit organizations kick off fund-raising drives. Girl Scout councils begin their annual cookie sale in March. It is an opportunity to sell and eat boxes of yummy cookies on

The teachers of the new age

implore the sacred human race to awaken.

May we fulfill our sacred destiny

To be the sons and daughters of the cosmic light.

—Mayan Equinox Blessing

Do all the good you can,
By all the means you can,
In all the ways you can,
In all the places you can,
At all the times you can,
To all the people you can,
As long as ever you can.
—The Wesley Grace

behalf of a worthy organization. March also brings the first charity walks, runs, and bicycle rides of the year. Exercising for a good cause is a great way to burn off extra winter "insulation" and to get out and enjoy the warmer weather. The first taste of giving is often addictive; our actions in March remind us that it feels good to share our time, money, and energy with those in need.

The spring equinox also marks the arrival of **Norouz**, or the Persian New Year. Norouz celebrations date back to the ancient Assyrians, who gave gifts to the king on the first day of spring. Today, Muslims celebrate Norouz with prayers and rituals that commemorate the rebirth of life. At the break of dawn, Muslims gather at a local mosque for morning prayer. After the service, the mood is playful and joyous. Muslim families warmly greet each other and exchange good wishes and plates of food. Children hop from relative to relative to offer hugs and to receive gifts of money. Afterward, family and friends gather for a special meal known as the haft-sinn or "seven Ss." Since seven is considered a lucky number in Persian folklore, the meal includes seven significant foods: *sabzeh* (home-grown sprouts), *samanou* (wheat germ), *sib* (apples), *sonbol* (hyacinth), *senjed* (jujube fruit), *seer* (garlic), and *somagh* (sumac). For Muslims, the first day of spring is a joyous time in which to reawaken their love of family, community, and God.

As we work towards that vision of the future,
We will remember the Sura of Light.
It tells us that the oil of the blessed olive tree
lights the lamp of understanding,
a light that belongs neither to East nor West.
In that spirit, all that we learn will belong to the world.
—His Highness Prince Karim Aga Khan

Buddhists also observe a special holiday in March called **Magha Puja**. Unlike other spring holidays that celebrate the return of the sun, Magha Puja celebrates the light within. On the first full moon of the month, Buddhists recite sutras and mantras to commemorate the spontaneous gathering of 1,250 enlightened saints (all of whom were ordained by Buddha himself) to pay their respects to their leader. Revered for renouncing his worldly goods, attaining enlightenment, and then dedicating his life to serve others, the Buddha epitomizes selfless service. On this day, many Buddhists engage in *metta*, or prayers of loving kindness. During a *metta* meditation, Buddhists offer heartfelt prayers to loved ones and adversaries alike. The prayer serves as a reminder to love every sentient being without any limitations.

If you knew, as I do,
the power of giving,
you would not let a single meal pass
without sharing some of it.
—Buddha

The spirit of renewal and rebirth in March also inspires sacred purification rituals such as **Ramadan** and **Lent**. Ramadan is a floating holiday that takes place in the ninth month of the Muslim lunar year (and therefore moves through all four seasons of the Gregorian calendar). Lent is a forty-day period of abstention and prayer observed by Christians. Since both festivals turn our attention inward and test our physical resolve, Lent and Ramadan are both described in the same month.

Ramadan celebrates the revelation of the Holy Koran and begins with **Layla-tul Qadr** meaning "night of [spiritual] power." On this night, Muslims begin a period of purification. The fast is extensive and rigorous —Muslims are forbidden to eat, drink, smoke, or engage in sexual relations between sunrise and sunset. Each evening after sunset, a special feast is prepared to break the fast. The intention of fasting is to remove one's anger and to evoke one's goodness. Muslims also believe that purified souls are the best vessels for divine inspiration, so those who fast also refrain from

Fasting is our sacrifice, it is the life of our soul;
Let us sacrifice all our body, since the soul has arrived as a guest.
Fortitude is as a sweet cloud, wisdom rains from it,
Because it was in such a month of fortitude that the Koran arrived.
—Jalal al-Din Rumi

dishonesty, stealing, or other unethical behavior. At the end of the monthlong fast, Muslims celebrate **Eid al-Fitr**, or the "Day of Feasting." On Eid, when Muslims officially conclude a month of abstention and humility, the mood is joyous. More than anything else, the fast reminds Muslims to appreciate every morsel of food and drink that they receive from Allah.

For the Mohamed family, Ramadan is a time to spend with loved ones. In the evenings, they invite friends and family to their home to break the daily fast. Before the evening meal, they bow their heads and recite a simple Muslim blessing. During the meal, grandparents and great- aunts recount parables from the Koran to grandchildren, nieces, and nephews. Afterward, everyone retires to the living room to discuss the changing face of Islam and peace in the Middle East. Through-out Ramadan, the Mohameds feel a greater sense of unity and solidarity with all human beings—regardless of their culture or religious background.

Bismillah, ar-Rahman, ar-Rahim

(In the name of Allah, the most beneficent, the most merciful.)

—Traditional, Muslim

Similar themes underlie the Christian Lenten season, which begins on **Ash Wednesday** and concludes forty days later on **Easter Sunday**. More broadly speaking, Lent is a time to retell, relive, and reflect upon Christian resurrection stories. During Lent, Christians are encouraged to refrain from eating certain foods, a practice that was inspired by Jesus'

Blessed are the poor in spirit: for theirs is the kingdom of heaven.

Blessed are they that mourn: for they shall be comforted.

Blessed are the meek: for they shall inherit the earth….

Blessed are the merciful: for they shall obtain mercy.

Blessed are the pure in heart: for they shall see God.

—From the Sermon on the Mount, Matthew 5:3-8

retreat into the wilderness for a forty-day fast. Many choose to give up something that they love during Lent; some abstain from eating rich foods, while others refrain from playing video games or watching movies. The most important aspect of this tradition is to live with greater restraint than during the rest of the year.

Since Lent also marks the last days of Jesus' life, many also read the Bible during or after the evening meal. A popular and evocative reading is the Sermon on the Mount; it beautifully summarizes the spirit of generosity embodied by the teachings and actions of Jesus.

Ash Wednesday, the first day of cycle, serves as a reminder of human mortality. After church service, ashes are dabbed on people's foreheads, echoing the biblical passage "Ashes to ashes, dust to dust." The Easter season continues for five weeks and then concludes with Holy Week—a time of reflection upon the crucifixion and resurrection of Christ. Throughout Lent, Ginny Cunningham, who recently rediscovered her love of the Catholic faith, practices a traditional Catholic ritual—reciting a blessing before and after the evening meal.

Many cultures also celebrate coming-of-age rituals in spring. The White Mountain Apache Indians of Arizona mount a four-day **Sunrise Dance** for pubescent girls. Each wears an eagle feather (representing long life), an abalone shell (representing Changing Woman, Mother of the Apache), and a buckskin gown. Once dressed in ceremonial costume, they dance under a teepee frame with the hope that each girl will always have a home in the community. Similarly, young Burmese men participate in **Shinbyu** ceremonies in March. Local monks shave their

Bless us, O Lord, and these Thy gifts
Which we are about to receive from Thy bounty
Through Christ our Lord. Amen.
—Catholic Blessing Before the Meal

We give Thee thanks, O Almighty God, for these Thy benefits
Who lives and reigns, world without end.
May the souls of the faithful departed,
Through the mercy of God, rest in peace. Amen.
—Catholic Blessing After the Meal

heads and dress in yellow robes before they are accepted into the monastery. Each boy stays for a short period of time, from a few days to a few months, before rejoining the community. For the Apache and Burmese peoples, the month of March symbolizes growth—an evolution that equally applies to humans and the natural world.

Shivaratri is a floating Hindu holiday that is usually celebrated in March. A solemn festival, Shivaratri is devoted to the worship of Shiva, the most powerful of the Hindu deities. Shiva is known as the Creator and Destroyer, a deity with a command over life and death. In the context of Shivaratri, darkness symbolizes ignorance. So, Hindus light candles, bonfires, and lanterns in order to welcome Shiva's light into their lives. In some parts of the Himalayas, Indian villagers pray and make offerings around blazing bonfires. The villagers keep them lit until the first light of morning. On a clear night, bonfires of Shivaratri dot the landscape for miles in every direction.

O Lord! You are a vivifying power of love,
Radiant illumination, and divine grace.
We pray for the divine light to illuminate our minds.
—From the Gayatri Mantra

The word *mantra* means "sacred utterance" in Sanskrit. According to Indian tradition, a mantra is a sacred word or set of words repeated at great length. To utter a mantra is to create an intimate bond with God and to still the mind through simple, repetitive prayer. The oldest and most famous of all mantras is the single syllable *om*—an expression of the divine word in its purest form. For more than three thousand years, Hindus have been reciting mantras to sing the praises of the Creator. On Shivaratri, mantras recalling the spirit of Shiva are recited while stoking the sacred fires.

March 8 is **International Women's Day** (IWD), a day to honor women's work in and outside of the home. Unlike Mother's Day, IWD was born out of the struggle to achieve women's equality. On March 8, 1857, female garment and textile industry workers in New York City protested unfair treatment of women. The protests began a march toward a national holiday in honor of women's work. As the suffragist movement expanded to include workplace issues, more and more women supported the idea for a women's work holiday. A landmark moment arrived in 1945, when the United Nations Charter became the first international agreement to proclaim gender equality as a fundamental human right. Even still, support for the idea dwindled in subsequent years. Nearly two decades later, the women's movement of the sixties rescued the idea but stripped it of its socialist associations. Finally, the UN agreed to sponsor the first official IWD in 1975.

In the 1970s, Molly Murphy MacGregor and a group of women from the Sonoma County Commission on the Status of Women initiated Women's History Week. First celebrated in 1978 in California, it later expanded into the National Women's History Project and a full month of gender education. During National Women's History Month, women share stories and lead discussions about the women's movement and gender issues. Ellie, a mother of three daughters, dedicates an evening in March to studying illustrious female leaders such as Eleanor Roosevelt and Harriet Tubman. She also reads excerpts from feminists such as Germaine Greer, Gloria Steinem, bell hooks, and Naomi Wolf before the evening meal.

By the middle of the month, the color green materializes everywhere—store windows, hats, and even pitchers of beer! Established in Ireland but celebrated across the globe, **Saint Patrick's Day** takes

Here, my daughters,
Is where love will be seen:
Not hidden in corners,
But in the midst of occasions of falling.
And even though there may be more faults,
And even some slight losses,
Our gain will be incomparably greater.
—Saint Teresa of Avila

I have met brave women who are exploring
the outer edge of human possibility,
with no history to guide them,
and with a courage to make themselves vulnerable
that I find moving beyond words.
—Gloria Steinem

place on March 17. Patrick, the son of a Roman official in fifth-century Britain, was originally brought to Ireland as a slave and spent many years working as a shepherd. Upon his return to Britain, he studied to become a priest. Eventually, he was appointed a bishop and traveled to Ireland to bring Christ's message to the Irish people. An intuitive teacher, Patrick transformed many pagan customs to reflect Christian beliefs and teachings. Stories abound of his using ordinary objects—such as the shamrock—to teach the Irish about the Holy Trinity. Patrick is said to have founded more than three hundred churches and baptized more than one hundred twenty thousand people. The Roman Catholic church declared him a saint after his death.

Saint Patrick's Day is celebrated in many different ways: preparing a traditional meal of Irish stew, soda bread, corned beef, and cabbage; wearing green clothing; and marching in an annual Saint Patrick's Day parade. These celebrations can be boisterous, but Irish historians and theologians like to remind people that Patrick's legacy was built from serving humanity, not pitchers of beer. On this day, many Irish families recite a special blessing for Saint Patrick and their cherished homeland.

May the Irish hills caress you.
May her lakes and rivers bless you.
May the luck of the Irish enfold you.
May the blessings of Saint Patrick behold you.
—Traditional, Irish

Two floating holidays on the Hebrew calendar, **Purim** and **Passover**, are celebrated either in March or April. Purim is a joyous holiday when Jews share baked goods, sumptuous foods, and gifts with one another. The holiday invites Jews to remember the time in history when Haman, an advisor to the king of Persia, tried to convince the king to slaughter all Jews. The drawing of lots, or purim, was used to determine the date of execution. Fortunately, Queen Esther, who was a Jew but had kept her heritage a secret, convinced her husband to save the Jews; he decided to execute his devious advisor instead. Today,

Purim is celebrated with two different traditions: *matanot laevyonim*, meaning "offering gifts to the poor," and *mishloach manot*, meaning "giving gifts to friends and family." On Purim, Jews either offer a meal or enough money for a meal to someone in need. Then they visit friends and family bearing plates of food. Finally, after giving gifts to others, they too partake in a festive meal. The Hart family recites an excerpt from the Kaddish, a blessing for those who have passed away, to commemorate the death of their ancestors.

Let us bless and let us extol,
Let us tell aloud and let us raise aloft,
Let us set on high and let us honor,
Let us exalt and let us praise the Holy One—
Blessed be He!
—From Kaddish Prayer

Purim is also known as "Jewish Halloween." One of the most entertaining customs of the holiday involves dressing up in masks and costumes and attending Purim parties. Queen Esther, who concealed her Jewish identity and was thereby able to save her fellow Jews, likely inspired this custom. Celebrants often assume one of the characters found in the Book of Esther, such as King Ahasuerus, Queen Esther, Mordecai, and the evil Haman, or dress up as people whom they admire for their morality, courage, and tenacity. For children, the highlight of the Purim party is the moment when the winner of the costume contest is announced amidst great fanfare!

Passover is celebrated for eight days beginning on the fifteenth day of the Hebrew month of Nisan. The word *seder* means "order" and refers to the order of historical events recalled during the Passover meal. During the meal, each person takes a turn reading from the Haggadah—a collection of literary works including biblical passages, psalms, prayers, blessings, and stories. The fifteen steps, beginning with passages recalling slavery and ending with those evoking freedom, include tasting special Passover foods dipped in salt water. While the Haggadah is read at Passover dinners throughout the world, every family or community usually develops its own customs and rituals surrounding Seder. Jenny and Kenneth compiled

Blessed are you, our God,
Creator of the universe,
Who has kept us in life,
And sustained us,
And enabled us to reach this festive season.
—From the Passover Haggadah

their own Haggadah after getting married; they performed extensive research and then selected translations and verses that appealed to their personal beliefs.

After reading the Haggadah, everyone engages in a meal comprised of symbolic foods—such as unleavened bread (*matzoh*), bitter herbs, and hard-boiled eggs—that symbolize the hardship and sacrifices endured by the Jews. The Fulop family celebrates Passover by inviting friends and neighbors—of all backgrounds—to partake in the meal. A family of intellectuals, they encourage everyone to discuss the Haggadah, the seder, and the significance of Passover. The constant refilling of wine glasses usually leads to lively debate, analysis, and story telling at the dinner table!

In March, we shed outer garments—winter coats, sweaters, and boots—and allow our skin to breathe again. Feeling light and free without bulky garments, we run, play, and walk outdoors, appreciating the feel of the sun, rain, and wind on our skin.

May we listen when others speak;
May we remain sensitive to another's pain;
May we give up our time, energy, and possessions,
without contemplation or hesitation,
when called to serve a fellow human being.
—Taz Tagore

APRIL: *Awakening of the Earth and Ourselves*

The word April is derived from the Latin word *aprilis*; interpretations of the meaning range from "to open," to "love," and "full of sunlight." It is the month when the earth undergoes a transformation akin to adolescence. April is an awkward month: long periods of rain are followed by short growth spurts. April rains are heavy, warm, and cleansing—they help coax seeds out of the earth and transform them into shapely plants and flowers. It is fitting, then, that April's holidays are focused on expressing appreciation for the planet. In April we rejoice in the natural awakening of the earth's rivers, mountains, seas, and sky.

O Lord, bless the waters of the river.
Gladden the face of the earth.
May her furrows be watered, her fruits multiply;
Prepare it for seed and harvest.
  —Traditional, Egyptian

After a long winter, April's sights and sounds are a feast for the senses. Sunny yellow daffodils beckon us to lean in to take a closer look. Bees begin their migration from flower to flower, their wings working fast enough to create a pleasant buzz in the air. Frogs create a nightly symphony of peeps, trills, and whoops. In the countryside, newly born calves, lambs, and kids frolic in the sprouting grasses. Watching the birth of new life in April reminds us of our own humble beginnings.

The old adage, "April showers bring May flowers," helps us remember to embrace the damp weather. Ancient Chinese poems describe April rains as fine silk unraveling from the sky. For some, the rains have a calming effect; for

I am the one whose praise echoes on high.
I adorn all the earth.
I am the breeze that nurtures all things green.
I encourage blossoms to flourish with ripening fruits.
I am led by the spirit to feed the purest streams.
I am the rain coming from the dew
that causes the grasses to laugh with the joy of life.
I am the yearning for good.
—— Hildegard of Bingen

Blessing is like the spiritual bloodstream
that flows through the universe.
When we bless something, we are returning
what we have received to its source.
—Brother David Steindl-Rast

others, it inspires playful mischief such as puddle jumping, splashing, and umbrella tipping. April is the perfect month in which to don a bright yellow raincoat and dark galoshes and investigate a local garden or park. In April, everything around us—the air, wind, and soil—smells of rain. At night, the soft pitter-patter of raindrops on our windowpanes lulls us into a deep slumber.

In terms of holidays, April begins with a nudge and a wink. **April Fool's Day** was born out of Pope Gregory XIII's decision to replace the Julian calendar with the Gregorian calendar. For the millions who celebrated the New Year on April 1, adapting to a new calendar was difficult. The early adopters ridiculed those who clung to the old ways, calling them "April fools." In the mid-eighteenth century, after Great Britain adopted the Gregorian calendar, April Fool's Day became popular in England and the American colonies. This day is celebrated with pranks of all sorts. College newspapers print fake stories, tricksters change the time on clocks, and some even delight in rearranging the furniture in a public space.

Blessed are we who can laugh
at ourselves
for we shall never cease
to be amused.
—Anonymous

On the first Sunday in April, **Daylight Saving Time** often causes further confusion. An idea first conceived by Benjamin Franklin in the eighteenth century, Daylight Saving Time was eventually embraced as a way to better utilize daylight. Its usefulness in agrarian economies (the extra daylight gave farmers and farmhands more time in which to plant and harvest crops), led to its adoption after World War I. At 2 a.m. on that April Sunday, we "spring ahead" by turning our clocks forward one hour. For those who forget to do so, a late arrival at Sunday brunch or church may result in feeling foolish twice in one month!

May all beings have happiness and the causes of happiness;
May all beings be freed from suffering and the causes of suffering;
May all beings never be parted from freedom's true joy;
May all beings dwell in equanimity, free from attachment and aversion.
—Traditional, Buddhist

An important April shower is the bridal shower—a tradition that came into being in the late nineteenth century. It is so named because a parasol filled with little gifts was turned upside down over the bride-to-be, "showering" her with gifts from her friends. From then on, the custom of throwing a bridal shower gained prominence. On these occasions, female friends of the bride and groom gather to toast the promise of marriage. Over glasses of wine and hors d'oeuvres, guests discuss the wedding plans or listen to stories about how the couple met and fell in love. Intimate gifts, such as lingerie and perfume, express our appreciation for the bride-to-be while simultaneously inducing a blush on her cheeks!

The giddiness of April is further fueled with the annual blossoming of Japanese cherry trees. Around the globe, people stroll and picnic amidst acres of cherry trees. In peak season, thousands of light pink blossoms open and shortly thereafter fall to the ground. Cherry blossom festivals are an ancient and delightful tradition in Japan. In some

The little space within the heart
is as great as this vast universe.
The heavens and the earth are there,
And the sun, and the moon, and the stars;
Fire and lightning and winds are there;
For the whole universe is in Him
and He dwells within our heart.
—The Upanishads

regions, crowds arrive early in the morning bearing picnic baskets and sporting robes, and even masks! Parties of amateur musicians playing the *shamisen* recapture the spirit of cherry blossom festivals from the Edo period. Seasonal haiku are written on small note cards and distributed to friends and family to celebrate the arrival of spring.

> *Live in simple faith*
> *just as this*
> *trusting cherry*
> *flowers, fades, and falls.*
> —Issa

The annual **Cherry Blossom Festival** in Washington, D.C., commemorates the 1912 gift of three thousand cherry trees from Mayor Yukio Ozaki of Tokyo. In subsequent years, gifts of flowering trees were exchanged between the two nations as a token of their growing friendship. In 1915, the United States government gave dogwood trees to Japan. In 1965, three thousand eight hundred trees were given to the U.S. In 1981, Japanese horticulturalists took cuttings from American cherry trees to replace those that had been destroyed in a flood. Nearly seventy years later, the cycle of giving came full circle. More than seven hundred thousand people visit Washington each year to admire the blossoms that symbolize the arrival of spring.

April is also a month to take notice of the toxins, pollutants, and extinction of natural species on the planet. **Earth Day**, celebrated on April 22, is dedicated to environmental education. In the late sixties, Senator Gaylord Nelson of Wisconsin sought to raise awareness about the state of the environment. By the early seventies, Earth Day was observed with protests, speeches, and concerts in cities across the U.S. Earth Day marked the birth of the contemporary environmental movement and the first time that America, as a whole, reflected on the state of the planet. Over time, Earth Day celebrations shifted to balance political protests with individual action. On Earth Day, we are encouraged to compost yard waste, join a car pool, or plant a tree. Many also recite special prayers drawn from Native American tribes, environmentalists,

> *The Earth, its life am I,*
> *The Earth, its feet are my feet,*
> *The Earth, its legs are my legs,*
> *The Earth, its body is my body,*
> *The Earth, its thoughts are my thoughts,*
> *The Earth, its speech is my speech.*
> — Navajo Chant

philosophers and poets. The blessings remind us that the earth's survival is conditional upon our respect and appreciation for its gifts.

Following close on the heels of Earth Day is **Arbor Day**—usually celebrated on the last Friday in April. It began on April 10, 1872, with the planting of over one million trees in Nebraska. Julius Sterling Morton, the de facto founder of Arbor Day, established a special day to educate the whole country about the depletion of forested land. His efforts inspired a national holiday, when Americans are encouraged to support reforestation by planting trees, bushes, and other foliage. For millennia, trees have been important literary and metaphorical symbols: A tree's longevity inspires associations with immortality, and its roots often symbolize connections to the under-world. Trees also protect us from rain and sun, pro-vide a resting place for a nap or picnic, and supply us with fresh fruits, flowers, and firewood. For all these reasons, Arbor Day is a good time to reach out and praise wood!

Let us endeavor then by our words on Arbor Day,
And all other opportune occasions
To so embellish the world with plant life, trees, flowers, and foliage,
As to make our earth homes approximate
To those which the prophets, poets, and seers of all ages
Have portrayed as the Home in Heaven.
—Julius Sterling Morton, Address on Arbor Day

Visakha Puja, the Buddha's birthday, is the most important Buddhist festival. On April 8, Buddhists honor the birth, enlightenment, and death of the Buddha. Most Buddhist festivals are joyful occasions when people visit a local temple, chant beautiful passages from the Lotus Sutra, and listen to a Dharma talk. Some Buddhists prepare special foods on Visakha Puja and offer them to the monks and nuns. Buddhists are encouraged to help others on the Buddha's birthday by volunteering at a local charity to serve food or administer medical care to the needy.

Local temples have developed many unique rituals for Visakha Puja. In some temples, sweet tea is poured upon a statue of the baby

So within yourself let grow
A boundless love for all creatures.
Let your love flow outward through the universe,
To its height, its depth, its broad extent,
A limitless love, without hatred or enmity.
Then as you stand or walk, sit or lie down,
As long as you are awake,
Strive for this with a one-pointed mind;
Your life will bring heaven to earth.
—Buddha

Siddhartha, recalling the legend that sweet tea rained down from the skies when the Buddha was born. Another traditional custom involves lighting and dedicating a lantern. This ceremony encourages Buddhists to renew their commitment to attain, and to help others attain, enlightenment. Lantern dedications range from praying for the happiness of all beings to seeking guidance to overcome a personal struggle. In most temples, the festival concludes with evening prayers and chants that reflect the Buddha's teachings and spirit of generosity.

The teachings, life, and sacrifice of Jesus are honored during Holy Week, which marks His last seven days on earth. On **Palm Sunday**, church services commemorate Jesus' triumphant return to Jerusalem with special prayers and the distribution of palm leaves. **Maundy Thursday** marks the Last Supper and Jesus' revelation of his betrayal by one of the twelve disciples. **Good Friday** is the anniversary of the Crucifixion, the day Christ died on the cross. **Easter Sunday**, the day Christ was resurrected, concludes Lent. Historically, Easter Sunday celebrations began with a sunrise service and were followed by an elaborate feast.

During Holy Week, the Bucko family replaces their mealtime prayers with a single gesture: the sign of the cross. For the Buckos, this simple motion is an expression of their faith in the Blessed Trinity. Early Christians enacted this simple ritual when they were in need of hope and strength. Tertullian, the third-century Christian, wrote that people made the sign of the cross before rising, entering, or leaving their houses, and before bathing, eating, and sleeping—it conveyed their constant remembrance of God.

Eostre is the name of an Anglo-Saxon goddess of the dawn who was represented by a hare. Every spring, pagan festivals honored Eostre because she was believed to bring increased daylight. Since Eostre festival coincided with Jesus' resurrection, the holiday was easily assimilated into the Christian Church. In 325 C.E., Emperor Constantine decreed that Easter would be celebrated on the first Sunday after the first full moon in spring. Easter is more than a single Christian holiday—it marks the beginning of a season of natural renewal.

The Easter hare, symbolizing fertility and growth, eventually morphed into the Easter bunny and hatched the Easter egg! The Germans brought the symbol of the Easter bunny to America; it was not incorporated into Easter traditions until after the Civil War. In the late nineteenth and early twentieth centuries, Easter evolved from an old religious holiday to a family-centered festival focused on children. Even still, most Christians attend church services on Easter Sunday. Contemporary traditions include wearing bonnets, creating flower baskets, and mounting huge parades.

Eggs have the perfect shape to fit inside a human hand, and they also represent rebirth during the Easter season. The practice of dyeing or painting eggs originated from spring festivals in Persia. Other variations of Easter eggs include ornamental eggs and the tastier store-bought chocolate versions. Czar Alexander of Russia asked the famous goldsmith Peter Fabergé to create a special Easter egg for his wife, the Empress Marie. Alexander's son Nicholas continued the tradition until the Russian Revolution brought an end to the czarist rule in the country. Now the

In the name of the Father,
And of the Son,
And of the Holy Spirit.
Amen.
—Sign of the Cross Blessing

O God, source of life,
Fill our hearts with the joys of Easter.
In Your goodness You have given us food to eat;
Grant that we may continue to live the new life
Which Christ has won for us
and graciously bestowed upon us.
—Traditional Easter Blessing

My fiftieth year had come and gone,
I sat, a solitary man,
In a crowded London shop,
An open book and empty cup
On the marble table-top.
While on the shop and street I gazed
My body of a sudden blazed;
And twenty minutes more or less
It seemed, so great my happiness,
That I was blessed and could bless.
—From "Vacillation," W. B. Yeats

Fabergé egg collection is an international treasure distributed among museums and private collectors. Easter eggs can also form the basis of outdoor activities such as egg hunts, egg tosses, and egg-painting contests. Prayers and blessings recited during the holiday evoke the spirit of the Easter egg: the promise of a new beginning.

The Taylor family mounts a special Easter Sunday gathering every year. During an early-morning church service, nearly forty members of their extended family meet at church to sing and pray. Upon returning home, they gather in the kitchen to chat, share stories, and prepare a feast. After a long and happy meal, everyone retires to the backyard for an evening of performances. The Taylors—a family of singers, comedians, musicians, and artists—put on Broadway-worthy performances that attract the attention (and applause) of neighbors and passersby.

Lovely Easter celebrations are a far cry from the poet T. S. Eliot's declaration that "April is the cruelest month." His words are often repeated in April as part of **National Poetry Month**. This celebration enables us to pay homage to ancient and contemporary verse, from Dante and Shakespeare to Yeats and Dr. Seuss. Talented poets amaze us with their ability to evoke profound emotions and powerful memories in so few words. A treasured poetry collection, including short verse, quatrains, haiku, and sonnets, is the perfect companion for a long April walk in the park. Bartholomew, a budding poet, enjoys

researching and reading poems appropriate for every season. In April, he likes to read poems with a sacred theme before the evening meal.

Outside, the beauty of springtime creates a different kind of poetry. While resting on a park bench, we might observe a bird taking flight, an apple blossom falling to the earth, or a butterfly spreading its wet wings after emerging from a cocoon. In that instant, April's poetry is visible to all who want to observe it.

Like the wings of a butterfly,
Help me display the colors of my soul.
Like the migration of a butterfly,
Help me travel great distances for freedom.
Like the purpose of the butterfly,
Help me spread the seeds of life.
Like the spirit of a butterfly,
Help me to ascend to the heavens
When my journey on earth is complete.
—Taz Tagore

MAY: *Blossoming and Transformation*

May. This one-syllable declaration of springtime is simple, serene, and unpretentious. Just saying the word evokes a burst of activity—May! Derived from the Latin word Maia, the Roman goddess of growth, the earth springs into motion in May—flowers blossom, eggs hatch, and rivers run quickly and freely. Following nature's lead, human beings catch "spring fever"—many jump out of bed before their alarm clocks buzz to take a morning stroll or work in the garden. It is also a social month; we host outdoor parties, dine al fresco, or take a camping trip. Indeed, May is a month for leaning forward and embracing the summer season.

Plant and nurture a single seed. Attend it daily. What blossoms before you will be a miracle. What blossoms within you may astonish you.

—Joyce McGreevy

Spring looks and feels like an evolving courtship. In April, the lingering rays of the sun invited shy displays like petals opening and tiny leaf buds sprouting. By early May, the sun bursts from the horizon at sunrise and quickly climbs into the sky. Flowers appear in open fields and window boxes, on lawns and roadsides. Historically, people went into the nearby woods to "bring home the May" by collecting garlands of flowers and foliage. It is a month that makes us fall in love with the earth all over again.

May Day, originally celebrated as a six-day festival from April 28 to May 3, honors Flora, the Roman goddess of spring. Romans seeded the May Day tradition throughout Europe. By the fourteenth century, the practice of cutting down a tree from the woods, dragging it home, and then setting it upright had become a Welsh tradition. Local villagers decorated this "maypole" with flowers and herbs, hung streamers, and then danced around it. In some communities, dancers spiraled clockwise and counterclockwise, gradually forming a tight nucleus of bodies and streamers in the center. May Day festivities were capped off by selecting a young woman who embodied the spirit of the festival to be crowned the May Queen.

Another ancient nature ritual involved circling around hawthorn trees, which blossom with perfect white flowers in May. To the Celts, the hawthorn represented a link between earth and heaven; they circled around the tree to bring good luck in the upcoming year. The Celts engaged in May Day rituals to align themselves with the natural world; they hoped their actions and prayers would bring them good luck.

Another May tradition is the annual spring cleaning. In the month of May, Roman temples were cleansed and purified; centuries later, the Brits had their chimneys swept clean in May. Chimney sweepers even joined English May Day processions with brooms in hand! Today, many seize the month of May to wash the drapes, steam-clean carpets, and dust every nook and cranny of their homes. The Baker family engages in a thorough spring-cleaning in the middle of the month. After clearing out the attic, forgotten closets, and boxes stashed in the basement, they host a yard sale. The proceeds are split in half: a portion is donated to charity, and the remainder is spent buying new plants and flowers for their garden.

> *The sage does not hoard.*
> *The more he does for others,*
> *The more he has himself;*
> *The more he gives to others,*
> *The more his own bounty increases.*
> —Lao Tzu

May is also the month of the famous **Kentucky Derby**. On the first Saturday in May, thousands gather to sip mint juleps while watching the finest thoroughbred horses and their jockeys compete in this one-and-a-quarter-mile race. The Derby, which features three-year-old horses often from Europe, the Middle East, and Japan, is the first leg of the Triple Crown. Though it may seem old-fashioned, the Kentucky Derby is a

O Great Earth Mother
We your adoring children invoke you,
Grant us O Gracious One
That you will accept the seed
That we are about to plant in you
That you may bring forth new life
With which to nurture and sustain us.
Blessed be!
—Pagan Blessing

May your belly never grumble,
May your heart never ache.
May your horse never stumble,
May your cinch never break.
—Traditional, American

. . . Oh Earth, my mother,
My heart is full of gratitude
Because of the abundance, the beauty, and the love
That you offer me each day;
I have nothing but myself to offer in exchange.
Make me become beautiful and loving,
So that by giving myself to you, I can serve all.
—Traditional, Quechua

great reason to pull out a silly hat and a sassy summer dress and behave as though summer has arrived!

The celebrations continue for **Cinco de Mayo**. This holiday commemorates the Mexican defeat of the French in the Battle of Puebla. Initially, the French sent troops to help the Mexicans collect taxes. Instead, they seized the opportunity to conquer Mexico for themselves. Cinco de Mayo celebrates the staving off of foreign invaders to retain Mexico's independence. The holiday is celebrated by feasting on Mexican foods such as spicy salsas, rich guacamoles, and tender tamales. After a day of parades, speeches, and feasting, mariachi bands make music in the spirit of freedom and liberty. Some bands play a rendition of "La Cucaracha," a crowd-pleasing song written during the Mexican Revolution. Olé!

Mother's Day, celebrated on the second Sunday in May, is a time to honor mothers and the myriad other women—grandmothers, aunts, and sisters—who raised us. The earliest tributes to mothers date back to Greek festivals dedicated to Rhea, the mother of many deities, and ancient Roman offerings to Cybele, the Great Mother of Gods. Historically, Christians celebrated their mothers on the fourth Sunday of Lent to honor Mary, mother of Christ. In seventeenth-century England, the holiday was expanded to include all mothers and named Mothering Sunday. It enabled servants and apprentices to go home and visit their mothers. By the end of the nineteenth century, the tradition had all but disappeared.

Approximately 150 years ago, Ann Reeves Jarvis, an Appalachian homemaker, organized a day to care for the wounded and raise awareness of poor health conditions in her community. She believed that mothers best advocated her cause so she called it "Mother's Work Day." After her

Observing any human being from infancy,

seeing someone come into existence,

like a new flower in bud,

each petal first tightly furled around another,

and then the natural loosening and unfurling,

the opening into a bloom,

the life of that bloom

must be something wonderful to behold.

—Jamaica Kincaid

death, her daughter, named Anna Jarvis, took up the cause and eventually succeeded in convincing Congress to establish an official Mother's Day in 1914. It has since taken root in America and abroad as a day on which to praise, serenade, and honor our mothers. Mother's Day is an opportunity to express appreciation for the nurturing we take for granted—our mothers' healing touch, generous instinct, and infinite patience.

Corey recently moved to New York City to be closer to her adoring mother. On Mother's Day she writes an appreciative letter to her mother and also sends notes to her grandmother and Aunt Ruthy filled with funny anecdotes from their shared experiences. Susan makes a point of driving to New Jersey on Mother's Day to treat her mom to a day of pampering at a local salon; afterward, they drink wine and eat a decadent meal together.

If we can't say the words in person, gorgeous flower bouquets communicate a message of love. Anna Jarvis began this tradition by offering carnations, her mother's favorite flower, on the first official Mother's Day. Today, flowers are synonymous with Mother's Day. Even in France, a cake resembling a bouquet of flowers is served on this day! Poeta, who lives far away from her mother, always sends a bouquet of flowers

My mother is everywhere . . .

In the perfume of a rose,

The eyes of a tiger,

The pages of a book,

The food that we partake,

The whistling wind of the desert,

The blazing gems of sunset,

The crystal light of full moon,

The opal veils of sunrise.

—Hindu Chant

accompanied by a heartwarming poem celebrating motherhood. In turn, her mother created a scrapbook filled with poems and dried flowers to commemorate the annual tradition.

Flowers assume a different meaning when set beside the graves of loved ones. On the last Monday in May, Americans celebrate **Memorial Day**. The day was originally set aside to honor the brave soldiers of the Civil War and was later expanded to include those who fought and died in any war. While Waterloo, New York, was officially declared the birthplace of Memorial Day in 1966, the holiday originated from small local gatherings to honor soldiers who had perished in battle. Eventually, these became prevalent enough to warrant a national holiday. At many of these gatherings, solemn speeches and poems are read aloud in honor of those who bravely served their country and fellow citizens.

Our dead brothers still live for us,
and bid us think of life, not death—
of life to which in their youth
they lent the passion and joy of the spring.
As I listen, the great chorus of life and joy begins again…
a note of daring, hope, and will.
—From 1884 Memorial Day Address, Oliver Wendell Holmes, Jr.

The birthdate of Queen Victoria, the majestic "British Mum," is celebrated on the Monday preceding May 24 in Britain and Commonwealth countries such as Canada and Australia. During and after Queen Victoria's life, her subjects celebrated her birthday to express their loyalty to the British Empire. Canadians began to celebrate the Queen's birthday in the early 1900s. In 1947, the holiday—first called Empire Day—was changed to the more agreeable Commonwealth Day and later to **Victoria Day**. Even after achieving independence from

Britain, Canadians celebrate Victoria Day with parades, barbecues, and the occasional visit from a member of the royal family. After all, who can resist toasting a living queen or princess?

The month of May reawakens our senses and boosts our spirits. Uplifted by the songs of returning birds and the intoxicating rays of the sun, we are filled with hope. Although January is the first month of the year, May feels like a new beginning—it is a time to initiate new projects, plan summer vacations, and set new aspirations. Bolstered by the vitality of the natural world, we dare to dream in the month of May.

Bless Her Majesty the Queen
A beloved presence
Dignified but never distant
Regal but never remote
Winning affection by giving affection.
And gaining honor by honoring others.
Amen.
—**Blessing for Queen Victoria**

Bless these hands.
Warmed by the rays of the sun;
Caressed by the petals of spring flowers;
Cleansed by the refreshing rains;
Inspired by the mysterious force;
Bless these hands
so that they may create, nurture, and play.
—**Taz Tagore**

Father's Day
Canada Day
Fourth of July
Bastille Day
Buddhist Lent

Summer

JUNE: *Sharing and Togetherness*

June is a sweet and sensuous month. It is the beginning of the summer season and a month ruled by Juno, the Roman goddess of marriage and family. In the tradition of Juno, many exchange vows of marriage in the month of June. It is also when we celebrate the end of the academic year by attending high school and college graduation ceremonies. A string of heartwarming wedding receptions, graduation dinners, and summer parties marks the passage of time in June. Up above, the spirit of Juno is reflected by June's first full moon, also known as the "honeymoon."

We thank You, God, for our food,
For rest and home and all things good,
For wind and rain and stars above,
But most of all for those we love.
—Contemporary, American

After the spring mating season, the birds and bees tend their newly hatched young in June. Robins flit around collecting food for their hungry brood. Every morning, choruses of birdcalls ring through the air: the robin scolding, the purple finch singing praise, and the thrasher offering instruction. From eggs deposited in tree branches cicadas emerge and lend their song to the chorus. On most June evenings, a symphony of summer sounds fills the air.

The dry June breezes carry the scents of flowers, freshly cut grass, and damp earth into our homes and beckon us outside. Statuesque red roses, playful dahlias, and sensuous lilies fill the air with a heavy perfume. While wandering through a park or along forested trails, we collect June wildflowers, perfect for pinning onto our hair, wrists, and lapels. In our backyards, trees and bushes are ready to be pruned. The clippings can be used to sprout new plants or made into distinctive flower arrangements for the home or office.

Around June 22, or the summer solstice, the waxing sun reaches its zenith, resulting in the longest day of the year. Solstice, derived from the Latin *solstitium*, means "stoppage of the sun." After reaching its apex, the sun moves so slowly that it appears to be at a standstill. The old Celtic calendar marked the quarter segments of the year on the firsts of May, August, November, and February. So, June 21 was regarded as the halfway point between two seasonal markers rather than the beginning of summer. Since the eighth century, the English have named June 21 "Midsummer's Day."

Historically, people built fires to mark the summer solstice; Midsummer's Night bonfires dotted the Irish countryside well into the nineteenth century. Farmers built solstice fires adjacent to their fields and then walked the periphery of their property with fiery torches to protect crops and cattle from evil spirits. Afterward, the ashes of solstice fires were scattered in the fields to encourage an abundant crop.

Swedes celebrate Midsommar by decorating buildings, homes, cars, and boats with twigs and flowers. The "midnight sun" in June burns brightly enough for the festivities to extend well past midnight. The summer solstice was also regarded as an important turning point in China. The Chinese believe that yin and yang forces are battling at this time of year. As such, the Chinese take a rest on the eve of the summer solstice and wait for yin and yang to establish a new equilibrium. Nearly every culture and religion has created a blessing to praise the life-giving force of the sun. Solstice blessings recall the role of the sun in awakening and sustaining new life.

In June we celebrate those graduating from high school or college. Seeing one's child, sibling, relative, or friend cross the stage in cap and gown inspires tremendous pride and joy. Alumni and valedictory addresses feature words of wisdom

What a wonderful world
You have made out of the wet mud,
And what beautiful men and women!
We drink in your creation with our eyes.
We listen to the birds' jubilee with our ears.
How strong and good and sure your earth smells,
And everything that grows there.
We thank you for the beauty of this earth.
—Ashanti Prayer

Look to the sun for it is life.
Its touch awakens flowers,
Stirs seeds from beneath the earth,
Beckons leaves from the branches of trees,
Adds a touch of gold to our cheeks,
And awakens the love in our hearts.
Bless the rays of the sun.
—Solstice Blessing

from philosophers, politicians, and captains of industry. The speeches invite everyone to reflect on the purpose and meaning of an education. They also remind us that graduation ceremonies mark the beginning, not the end, of a lifelong journey to become educated and compassionate people.

In June, large crowds gather to watch the spectacular Chinese **Dragon Boat Festival**. Dragon boat racing became popular in the Tang Dynasty (618-907 B.C.E.) and later spread to the Yangtze River Valley and southern China. The Dragon Boat Festival is the oldest and most popular Chinese holiday after Chinese New Year. The festival's origin is linked to Ch'ü Yuan, a Chinese statesman and scholar born in the fourth century B.C.E. Yuan was banished for speaking out against corruption in the kingdom and later wandered the countryside composing poetry. When he threw himself into the Mi-lo River, local villagers searched for his body in dragon boats, tossing rice dumplings in their path to appease the water spirits. Contemporary festivals continue the tradition of offering prayers to the spirits: Prior to the races, dragon boats are blessed into awakening, and then paper bills are burned to ward off evil spirits. On the day of the race, teams row their boats forward to the beat of a drum. One person typically stands in the boat searching for Ch'ü Yuan's body while the others paddle. The Dragon Boat Festival, a test of teamwork, coordination, and strength, resonates with the spirit of June.

June has long been a popular season for engagements and weddings. According to tradition, men proposed in June with the promise of getting married in one year and one day. Today, engagements occur year-round, although June remains a popular month for weddings. Many contemporary weddings are built upon age-old traditions such as formal wedding attire, wedding blessings, an exchange of vows, and the wedding reception.

I learned this, at least, by my experiment;
that if one advances confidently in the direction of his dreams,
and endeavors to live the life which he has imagined,
he will meet with a success unexpected in common hours.
—Henry David Thoreau

I have just three things to teach:
Simplicity, patience, compassion.
These three are your greatest treasures.
Simple in actions and in thoughts,
You return to the source of being.
Patient with both friends and enemies,
You accord with the way things are.
Compassionate toward yourself,
You reconcile all beings in the world.
—Lao Tzu

During the Middle Ages, European brides and grooms wore something blue, the color of purity. This tradition led to its inclusion in the phrase, "Something old, something new, something borrowed, something blue," which describes the contents of a bridal trousseau. It wasn't until 1499, when Anne of Brittany wore an all-white dress, that the custom changed. In the pagan tradition, white wedding gowns symbolize the goddess's sensuousness and loving nature. For Chinese and Indian weddings, the bride wears red, symbolizing happiness and prosperity. Today, wedding gowns are usually made from specialty silk or satin and are accompanied by veils and extensive trains. Historically, an elaborate gown was intended to ensure that all eyes—especially those of the groom—were on the bride!

Flowers, symbolizing fertility, new life, and youthful love, are ever-present at weddings. Before the fourteenth century, a bride carried a single flower or a few loose blossoms. Then, probably owing to a particularly fashionable aristocrat, a bouquet became de rigueur. Even the groom was encouraged to wear a flower represented in the bridal bouquet on his lapel. By medieval standards, a knight who bore his lady's colors on his chest had openly declared his love for her. Contemporary weddings usually include elaborate floral centerpieces and bouquets. According to an old English tradition, the bride tosses her bouquet to pass her good fortune to others. The woman who catches the bouquet is supposed to be next in line for marriage.

Historically, Roman law mandated that weddings be conducted in the presence of ten witnesses. According to Roman mythology, the presence of male and female witnesses—dressed in clothing resembling the bride and groom—confused evil spirits and prevented mischief during the ceremony. This tradition has continued into the present; most couples invite their closest friends and family members to join the wedding

The moment two bubbles
are united, they both vanish.
A lotus blooms.
—Kijo Murakami

Now you will feel no rain,
For each of you will be shelter for the other.
Now you will feel no cold,
For each of you will be warmth for the other.
Now there is no more loneliness,
For you are two persons with one life before you.
—Apache Wedding Prayer

The earth laughs in flowers;
A flower is love looking for a word.
—Traditional Verse

processional. Since weddings usually take place in a house of worship, prayers and blessings are often recited. Typically, there are two prayers during the wedding service: the invocation (at the beginning of the ceremony) and the wedding prayer (after the recitation of vows). The wedding prayer is recited by the priest, minister, or rabbi and is intended to shower sacred blessings upon the couple.

May your love cast out small fears.
May your hope summon tremendous courage.
May your faith in each other
and in this radiant universe
grow and flourish.
—Wedding Blessing

The recitation of wedding vows can be traced back to the Middle Ages. Originally intended as covenants to reinforce the sanctity of marriage, vows have evolved from standardized oaths to personal invocations of love and praise. The recitation of vows precedes the exchange of wedding bands. The Greeks believed that the third finger was connected to the heart by the vein of love. So it became the "ring finger" or the finger upon which the engagement and wedding rings were placed. Before the end of the ceremony, the officiating minister often recites a final inspirational reading drawn from a sacred text or a romantic philosopher. In Roman times, a kiss was considered a legal bond with the power to seal a contract. And so, with a kiss, two people are united in the spirit of love.

After the ceremony, showering the newlyweds with rice and confetti enacts an ancient fertility rite. The grains, representing life-giving seeds, were tossed to help the couple quickly conceive a child. The wedding reception, intended to signify the joining of two families, has evolved into a lavish affair. Elaborate cocktail receptions and meals enable families to officially welcome each other with toasts and good wishes. The first dance, typically offered to the bride and groom, enables the guests to admire the newlywed couple. Afterwards, a playful band or deejay coaxes guests out of their chairs and onto the dance floor to burn off all the wine and wedding cake.

May love be the foundation

Of how we live our lives together;

May our love radiate through our smiles

And shine through our eyes;

May we stand by each other

As a tree stands by a river—

Constant, loyal and steadfast;

May love fill our hearts and expand our minds;

May it help us believe

That we can do and be anything together.

—Adapted from the Wedding Vows of Jeff and Renee George

Having celebrated Mother's Day in May, we celebrate fathers in June. Sonora Smart Dodd of Washington State first proposed the idea of a "father's day" in 1909. She wanted to enact a special day to honor her father, a Civil War veteran who single-handedly raised six children after becoming a widower. The first father's day was observed on June 19, 1910 in Spokane, Washington. Coincidentally, in several cities across America, father's day celebrations had independently sprung up around the same time of the year. Then, in 1924, President Calvin Coolidge offered public support for a national father's day. The idea gained momentum until 1966, when President Lyndon Johnson signed a presidential proclamation declaring the third Sunday in June as **Father's Day**.

On this day, North Americans celebrate a father or father figure who played an important role in their lives. Father's Day is a time to tell our fathers that we need and appreciate them. For some, this sentiment calls for a practical gift such as a tie, book, or golf club. For others, Father's Day celebrations involve special meals and outings. Madeline was raised in California by her father; she takes her dad to a ballgame, where they eat hot dogs and popcorn, and cheer their favorite players. Sam spent much of his childhood turning down his father's offers to go spend a weekend in the wilderness. Now they always spend Father's Day weekend on a camping or fishing trip. As a gift, he sets up camp, cooks meals over the campfire, and tries not to catch a bigger fish than his dad.

The anniversary of the nonprofit organization Alcoholics Anonymous (A.A.) is celebrated on June 10. Founded in 1935, this international support group has helped millions of people achieve sobriety by offering them a path and a supportive community in which to heal. The organization encourages alcoholics to express themselves honestly in order to overcome their addiction. On this day, the two million members of the organization and their families celebrate the "Twelve Steps" that freed them from a life of dependency on alcohol.

There is no shortage of theories about the origin of the Saint Francis or Serenity Prayer, a blessing recited at the end of every local A.A. meeting. Records document that Dr. Reinhold Niebuhr (not Saint Francis), of the Union Theological Seminary, composed it in 1932. In 1934, Dr. Howard Robbins, a friend of Dr. Neibuhr, requested permission to include an abbreviated version of it in his book of prayers. A few years later, the cofounder of A.A. read it. He and the staff of the organization decided to print it on cards and passed them out to members. Today, the prayer is an anthem and call to action for those recovering from addiction.

Build me a son, O Lord,
Who will be strong enough to know when he is weak,
And brave enough to face himself when he is afraid;
One who will be proud and unbending in honest defeat,
And humble and gentle in victory.
—A Father's Prayer

God grant me the serenity
To accept the things I cannot change,
The courage to change the things I can,
And the wisdom to know the difference.
—Prayer of Saint Francis or Serenity Prayer

June also brings the Roman Catholic holiday **Corpus Christi**. On this day, Christians receive communion in observance of Jesus' Last Supper with the twelve disciples. Catholics living in all parts of the world celebrate this religious holiday by mounting elaborate parades and processions in their local towns. Prayers and sermons, centered upon the life and teachings of Jesus, inspire Christians to embody biblical teachings in their own lives. The Diaz family celebrates the holiday by furnishing an altar with candles, prayers, and porcelain figures of Jesus. The altar is kept intact for an entire year and is the center of their nightly family prayers.

Bless these thy gifts, most gracious God,
From whom all goodness springs;
Make clean our hearts and feed our souls,
With good and joyful things.
—Traditional, Christian

By the end of June, our bodies have acclimated to the balmy weather and communal spirit of the summer season. After a month of formal events and ceremonies, it feels great to trade in high heels for a pair of flip-flops, sandals, or clogs! In June, we develop "summer feet." After months of hiding our toes inside heavy socks, boots, and shoes, we allow our feet to breathe and to reconnect with the earth. June is the perfect time to walk barefoot in a local park, allowing our feet to sink down into the damp, cool, and ticklish grass.

Love is a choice. To choose it is to move purposefully towards our own or our beloved's spiritual growth. May this food supply us with the energy to act, to exercise free will, and to extend ourselves, for love.
—Taz Tagore

JULY: *Pursuing Adventure and Independence*

July is an exuberant month, with its joyful holidays proclaiming freedom and independence, and its bold colors, sounds, and flavors. In July we savor the fruits of life—food, family, and the beauty of nature—with all our senses. Many take time off to explore the lush countryside or go abroad to discover new places and people. No matter how far we travel in July, we're never more than a few miles from a local Independence Day parade or fireworks display. Whether we're overseas or at home, in July we reach out and grab life by the horns!

May we grant one another the opportunity to live out our dreams, to care for the wounded child in one another, and to pass on to others still unborn an earth as alive and diverse and wondrous as the one we have inherited.

— Matthew Fox

July is when we loosen the restrictions that guide our everyday lives and plunge into unknown territory. Some pack up the car, purchase a handful of maps, and embark on a long road trip. Others prefer to test their physical strength in the great outdoors by skydiving, parasailing over the ocean, or cycling through country roads and mountain trails. Children also catch July's spirit: many hit their first home run or take their first bicycle ride during summer vacation.

July is synonymous with people—crowds of people—from all walks of life. The balmy weather serves as the perfect backdrop for socializing. Plates of refreshing watermelon are always crowd-pleasers at family picnics and reunions—especially when they spur on seed-spitting contests. At a ball game, long lines at the hot dog stand inspire small talk among enthusiastic fans. And amusement parks are the only places where we can scream at the top of our lungs alongside complete strangers. Wherever we go in July, hundreds or even thousands have arrived first.

Instead of groaning about the fierce competition for refreshments and restrooms, we enjoy and celebrate our communities in July.

The heat and haze of July afternoons are occasionally interrupted by a sudden summer storm that rejuvenates wilting leaves and releases the fragrance of fresh herb gardens into the warm, moist air. In July, gardeners enjoy plucking and eating the first ripe tomato or basket of strawberries of the summer season. For the remainder of the summer, they will prune, clip, and nurture their gardens in anticipation of a lush summer harvest of sweet peas, zucchini, carrots, lettuce, green beans, and a variety of berries. Even the most experienced of them can't help but marvel at the miracle of the garden: by July, tiny seeds have matured into ripe fruits and vegetables.

Owing to the fresh supply of summer produce, we enjoy wonderful meals—cooked and eaten outdoors—in July. Gone are the days of craving rich, heavy foods; in July, we want fresh fruit, mixed green and vegetable salads, and grilled meats. With only a sharp knife, chopping board, and barbecue, we create perfect summer meals with very little effort. Similarly, summer blessings are often short and sweet. The Rhodes and Ostler families recite a quick grace when gathering on the backyard deck for a lively summer meal—they say the word "grace" and dig in!

The July holidays start with a bang! On July 1, Canadians celebrate **Canada Day**, a holiday that marks the nation's independence from Great Britain. The festivities on Parliament Hill showcase Canada's best artists, musicians, and comedians. It is also the day on which Canadians pay tribute to the aboriginal people who first settled the land. On this day,

May your hands always be busy,
May your feet always be swift,
May you have a strong foundation
When the winds of changes shift.
May your heart always be joyful,
May your song always be sung,
May you stay forever young,
Forever young, forever young,
May you stay forever young.
—From "Forever Young," Bob Dylan

For every cup and plateful,
God make us truly grateful.
—Traditional, American

God keep our land glorious and free!
O Canada, we stand on guard for thee.
O Canada, we stand on guard for thee.
—From "O Canada"

Canadians gather in backyards, public parks, and beaches to toast the distinctive spirit of the Canadian people. The beloved maple leaf is worn on hats and T-shirts and painted on the faces of the most boldly patriotic. Canadians often pause in the midst of an elaborate picnic or backyard party to sing the national anthem and salute their country's independence.

A few days later, Americans celebrate Independence Day. By the middle of the eighteenth century, England's thirteen colonies in the New World began to express their dissatisfaction about being ruled from afar and paying exorbitant taxes. The state of Virginia took the first step toward independence by voting to set up a committee representing the colonies. The First Continental Congress met in the fall of 1774. They drew up a list of grievances against the crown—the first draft of a document that would formally separate the colonies from England. George Washington took command of the Continental Army and marched against the British in Massachusetts. For the next eight years, colonists fought fervently in the Revolutionary War.

In the meantime, a war of words was being waged in Philadelphia. On July 2, 1776, the Second Continental Congress presented and debated a second draft of their grievances; John Hancock, the president of the Congress, was the first to sign the document, later renamed the Declaration of Independence. On July 4, the Second Continental Congress adopted the final draft of the document. Beginning on July 8 and continuing for a full month, the Declaration was read aloud to garner public support. In the following year, colonists rang bells, fired guns, and lit firecrackers in Philadelphia to celebrate American independence. Even though the war dragged on until 1783, Independence Day was made an official holiday in 1777. In the eighteenth

May we honor this nation that we call home.
May we live and work in a way
That sustains the land and its people.
May we recognize the true source
Of life, liberty, and the pursuit of happiness.
May we join together to create a nation
That embodies truth, justice, and freedom.
—Independence Day Blessing

century, church services were held after an important historic and political event. On Independence Day, many Americans attended church to sing and pray for the prosperity of the new nation.

Fourth of July celebrations are larger than life in many parts of America. It is a time to mount huge family picnics where hamburgers and hot dogs are eagerly consumed alongside potato salad, coleslaw, and corn on the cob. At the Stephens family picnic, everyone—regardless of age or ability—partakes in a fiercely competitive dodgeball tournament. The winner is served the first slice of red, white, and blue cake for dessert! The Masi family embarks on a camping trip every Fourth of July weekend. They spend Independence Day swimming in a lake, building sandcastles, and fishing. After an evening meal of fried fish, grilled corn, and "dump cake"—all prepared on a Coleman stove—the family lingers in and around their huge blue tent, waiting for night to fall.

Whose bread I eat,
His song I sing.
—Traditional, German

In some parts of the country, fireflies materialize out of the night sky in early July. Barbara, who grew up on Staten Island, remembers catching fireflies in a jar every Independence Day. Their faint glow was a sneak preview of the electrifying colors to come later in the evening. In cities and towns across America, the Fourth of July means FIREWORKS! From tiny handheld sparklers to exploding fireworks in the shapes of waterfalls, chrysanthemums, and roman candles, the skies above America thunder with smoke and sound on the Fourth of July.

O Master of the Earth,
You live without growing old.
You cover everything like the sky.
Give me the joy of understanding You,
As the earth and the sky understand You.
—Taoist Blessing

Many South American countries also celebrate their independence in July. On July 9, Argentineans celebrate the 1816 defeat of Spanish invaders. Holiday celebrations inevitably honor General José de San Martín, Argentina's greatest military hero and the leader of the fight for independence. On July 24, citizens of Bolivia, Colombia, Ecuador, Peru, and Venezuela celebrate the birth of Simón Bolívar. In 1819, Bolívar organized an army of 2,500 soldiers and marched through rivers and over the Andes to launch a surprise attack on the Spanish. After defeating the Spanish in what is now Colombia, he went on to liberate much of South America. Both holidays are celebrated with Latin American flair.

In some parts of Argentina, locals install hundreds of lanterns in public parks and plazas and then host huge outdoor barbecues for everyone in the vicinity. Since many Latin cultures share a love of prayer, family, and music, the Independence Day meals are prefaced with an expressive blessing recited by whoever feels most moved to say thanks. In the

> *Thank you, Lord, for cakes and other sweets;*
> *Thank you for those special dinners with the people we love,*
> *That make possible those unforgettable conversations;*
> *Thank you, Lord, for cold beer on hot days;*
> *Thank you for water, so simple, without flavor, but so good;*
> *Thank you, Lord, for lime sorbet, the taste of a kiss and the sharing of sex.*
> *For all the possibilities, Lord. Thank you.*
> —Contemporary, Latin America

evening, many eschew fireworks for a night of enthusiastic dancing with friends, neighbors, spouses, and children.

A celebration of independence wouldn't be complete without France. On July 14, the French celebrate **Bastille Day**. In the eighteenth century, French dissenters to the monarchy were locked up and punished at the Bastille prison. In 1789, the French people captured the Bastille, initiating the French Revolution. Eventually, their efforts led to the establishment of the first democratic Republic of France. Bastille Day celebrations reinforce democratic ideals such as liberty, equality, and brotherhood during parades and speeches. In typical French fashion, celebrants enthusiastically hug and kiss each other on the cheek, eat slabs of quiche and pungent *pissaladière* (anchovy tarts), and drink copious amounts of French wine. In the early evening, people dance to songs such as "La Marseillaise" or classic folk tunes played on an accordion. On Bastille Day, cobblestone streets throughout France are filled with merrymakers bursting with pride for their homeland.

There are thoughts which are prayers.
There are moments when,
whatever the posture of the body,
the soul is on its knees.
—From *Les Misérables*, Victor Hugo

The theme of independence is reflected in two different Tibetan Buddhist holidays observed in the month of July. On July 6, Tibetan Buddhists celebrate His Holiness the **Dalai Lama's Birthday**. The fourteenth Dalai Lama, currently living in exile in northern India, is the unofficial head of state of Tibet and the spiritual leader of a global community of Tibetan Buddhists. Since China annexed the country in 1951, Tibetans have lived under Chinese political rule but continue to recognize the leadership of past and present Dalai Lamas. "Dalai Lama" is a Mongolian title meaning "Ocean of Wisdom" and the fourteenth Dalai Lama was recognized as the manifestation of the bodhisattva of compassion at the age of two. In 1989, he was awarded the Nobel Peace Prize for leading a nonviolent struggle to liberate Tibet. He has consistently advocated policies of nonviolence, even in the face of extreme aggression. He also became the first Nobel laureate to be recognized for his concern for global environmental problems. Despite his notoriety, he describes himself as a "simple Buddhist monk" and teaches love, compassion, and forgiveness to others.

For as long as space endures
And for as long as living beings remain
Until then, may I too abide
To dispel the misery of the world.
—His Holiness the Dalai Lama

World Tibet Day, celebrated on July 3, was first celebrated in 1998. The holiday has three main goals: to create a worldwide event to help restore essential freedoms for the Tibetan people in occupied Tibet; to raise greater awareness of the genocidal threat to the Tibetan people; and to celebrate the unique beauty of Tibetan culture and thought. In recent years, World Tibet Day was observed in fifty-seven cities across the globe. For Tibetan Buddhists and general supporters of a free Tibet, this is a day in which to pray for freedom and justice in the world.

Before the introduction of Tibetan Buddhism in the seventh century C.E., most Tibetans followed the Bon religion, a shamanistic practice. Bon shamans had been making and hanging flags in the five colors, representing the five elements, believing they would offer protection. As Buddhism blended with Bon, sacred mantras and iconographies were painted onto the Bons' flags, creating what are known as Tibetan prayer flags. Prayer flags are raised to mark auspicious occasions such as the Dalai Lama's birthday and the Tibetan New Year. Tibetans believe that the wind carries the prayers off the cloth and into the heavens. It is common to write a person's name, a birth date, or short message on the flag to personalize it. Others inscribe the teachings of the Buddha on a prayer flag in the hopes of spreading his wisdom to all corners of the earth.

Now may every living thing,
Young or old,
Weak or strong,
Living near or far,
Known or unknown,
Living or departed or yet unborn,
May every living thing be full of bliss.
—Buddha

July's exuberance extends beyond the earth's atmosphere. On July 20, we celebrate the first-ever successful moonwalk by Neil Armstrong and Edwin Aldrin, Jr. On that day in 1969, the two American astronauts walked the surface of the moon, planted the American flag, and collected moon rocks for scientific research. Afterward, Armstrong's words of hope, "One small step for man, one giant leap for mankind," inspired generations of astronauts, rocket scientists, and science fiction buffs to research and contemplate outer space. Many famous astronauts and

But I did not fall....
Gravitation had become
as sovereign as love.
The earth, I felt,
was supporting my back,
sustaining me, lifting me up,
transporting me through
the immense void of night.
—From Wind, Sand, and Stars, Antoine de Saint-Exupéry

aviators have written ethereal poetry and prose about soaring through space. Their words assume a sacred tone when read aloud, resembling the cadence and passion of prayer.

July is especially delightful for children. For many, it is synonymous with summer camp activities such as swimming in a lake, sleeping in a tent, and singing songs around the campfire. Occasional complaints about insect bites and sunburn are eclipsed by the joy of spending a week, a

Thank you, thank you, thank you, Lord
For all the food we eat.
And it's so very nice of you,
To make some of it sweet.
—Girl Scout Campfire Grace (sung to the tune of "Row, Row, Row Your Boat")

month, or the whole summer outdoors. For children, July is a time to meet new friends, acquire new skills, and to embark on new adventures. Children grow stronger—in body and spirit—in the month of July.

Mealtime blessings take on a livelier and more playful spirit at summer camp. Many instructors encourage children to write blessings to match the tunes of their favorite nursery rhymes or campfire songs. Some blessings are sung in rounds until everyone is ready to eat; others are sung softly and solemnly while holding hands.

In Japan, children celebrate **Tanabata** on July 7. This popular Japanese festival is based upon a Chinese myth that a flock of magpies connected the constellation of lovers named Vega and Altair. Over time, the festival evolved into a day when children write poetry on long strips of paper and tie them to tree branches. The festival also invites

Thanks to God, for our food,
For our milk, for our stew, for our bread.
God is joy, God is love,
Bow your head.
—Girl Scout Campfire Grace (sung to the tune of "Taps")

Every day we are engaged in a miracle which we don't even recognize:
a blue sky, white clouds, green leaves, the black, curious eyes of a child—our own two eyes.
—Thich Nhat Hanh

May the lamp of love which eternally burns
Kindle divine fire in our hearts,
Opening our eyes and consuming our differences,
driving the shadows from our faces.
May we learn to love one another
Even better than we love ourselves.
—Lama Surya Das

children to hang earthly and celestial decorations of flowers, trees, animals, and stars to symbolize the ever-present link between heaven and earth.

A more solemn holiday, **Buddhist Lent**, which begins with the waning moon of the eighth lunar month, usually coincides with the rainy season in Southeast Asia. Historically, the Buddha cautioned monks not to leave their monasteries during the rainy season to prevent damage to budding rice plantations. In some parts of Asia, the beginning of Buddhist Lent is marked with a candle procession that ends at a local temple. Thousands gather to ceremoniously walk along the path from the center of town to the temple to make small offerings to the monks. However, since monks vow to own only eight possessions—undergarments, a robe, a belt, a begging bowl, a blade, a needle, a mat, and a water strainer—gift giving is limited to bare necessities. Many Buddhist followers find inspiration in the words of the Buddhist monks Lama Surya Das, Chögyam Trungpa Rinpoche and Pema Chodron, which are read aloud during prayer ceremonies and dharma talks, to strictly observe the five Buddhist precepts during Lent.

After a month of adventure, the weather in late July is too warm and humid to keep up the frenzied pace. Instead, we seek relief by turning on air conditioners and fans and preparing pitchers of sweet iced tea and lemonade. At night, some beat the heat by sleeping on enclosed porches, rooftops, or a flat stretch of sandy beach. Sleeping under the stars in July embodies the joie de vivre of the month—it is a time to commune with the luminescent skies and singing night owls before drifting off to sleep.

When we count our many blessings,
It isn't hard to see,
That life's most valued treasures,
Are the treasures that are free.
For it isn't what we own or buy,
That signifies our wealth.
It's the special gifts that have no price:
Our family, friends, and health.
—Author Unknown

Oh, the wonder of joy!
. . . From joy all beings have come,
By joy they all live,
And unto joy they all return.
—The Upanishads

May we heed the call of a bird
By sharing our distinct voice
And listening to the songs of others.
In doing so, may we take flight and soar
Among those who sing.
—Taz Tagore

Deep peace of the running wave to you,
Deep peace of the flowing air to you,
Deep peace of the quiet earth to you,
Deep peace of the shining stars to you,
Deep peace of the gentle night to you,
Deep peace of the Son of Peace to you,
Moon and stars pour their healing light on you,
Deep peace to you.
—Traditional, Gaelic

AUGUST:
Delighting in Rest and Leisure

The hot, lazy days of August give rise to a different rhythm of life. At work, at home, and at play, everyone and everything moves more slowly. Many spend the weekends by the sea or frolicking in a shimmering pool of water. The early morning and late evening, before and after the sun reaches its apex, are just cool enough for a long bike ride or run through the countryside. Despite the heat, August is also a sensuous month. A long, unbroken stream of ice cream truck jingles, fruit and vegetable harvests, and ice-cold glasses of lemonade marks the passage of time. And most enjoy this month of leisure without feeling a hint of remorse.

August days are hot and sticky enough to merit frequent showers, swims, or sprints through the backyard sprinkler to cool off. The brief afternoon thunderstorms explode in the expansive sky and rapidly soak everything in sight. The giant drops of water bounce off windshields and sidewalks with tremendous force. Shortly thereafter, they flee the skies and are replaced by the bright glare of the sun. August thunderstorms serve as a giant broom—sweeping out the humidity and momentarily bestowing upon us a warm, dry breeze. In August, all living things are at the mercy of the hot sun and the cloudless sky.

Food is not merely something we eat. . . . Eating is life.
Each time we eat,
the soul continues its earthly journey.
With every morsel of food swallowed a voice says,
"I choose life,
I choose to eat, for I yearn for something more."
—From a poem by Marc David

In the meadows, fields, and roadsides, a fresh crop of wildflowers and herbs emerges in the month of August. Miles of goldenrod, Queen Anne's lace, and milkweed pass before our eyes during long car

All of us have had the sudden experience of joy
that came when nothing in the world
had forewarned us of its coming—
a joy so thrilling that if it was born of misery
we remembered even the misery with tenderness.
—From *Wind, Sand, and Stars*, Antoine de Saint-Exupéry

trips. After producing succulent blossoms for many months, rosebushes and sunflower stalks dry out in the hot sun. After the loud birdsongs of July dissipate, other voices fill the summer air. Cedar waxwings gathered in dense berry thickets impart their high-pitched, wavering call against a backdrop of crickets. The soft blanket of natural sounds in August is occasionally punctuated with the sharp call of a bluejay or a hungry hawk.

After months of producing fresh produce, gardeners turn over beds of earth for a rest. However, the heat does not discourage the hardy tomato plant—the tomato harvest reaches its peak in August. The plump, juicy fruits invite us to eat them like apples, allowing the seeds and juice to dribble down our chins. Farther afield, orchards yield fleshy peaches, nectarines, and plums. They are the perfect size and shape to toss inside beach bags and purses; in the late afternoon, they supply a refreshing burst of energy and sweetness. At the dinner table, August blessings sing the praises of the fresh, tantalizing foods that supply life-giving energy to our bodies.

The slow pace of August lulls us into a groggy state. The hot sun and heavy air encircle us like a pair of heavy drapes. For many, August feels like a long string of afternoon

Lord of the World,
Bread from the earth sustains us
Wine gladdens our heart
And oil makes our faces shine.
May you be blessed
For these precious gifts that come from You
For our comfort and fulfillment.
—Italian Blessing

Bless our hearts,
To hear in the breaking of bread,
The song of the universe.
—Benedictine Blessing

Kum ba ya, my Lord, Kum ba ya.
Kum ba ya, my Lord, Kum ba ya.
Kum ba ya, my Lord, Kum ba ya.
Oh, Lord, Kum ba ya.
Someone's crying, Lord, Kum ba ya.
Someone's laughing, Lord, Kum ba ya.
Someone's shouting, Lord, Kum ba ya.
Someone's praying, Lord, Kum ba ya.
Kum ba ya, my Lord, Kum ba ya.
—Contemporary Folk Song

Bless every moment of this day.
Because yesterday is already a memory,
And tomorrow is only a dream.
We pray for the audacity to embrace this day.
—Taz Tagore

naps from which to awaken feeling disoriented but happy. For those seeking refuge by the seaside, a towel, sunscreen, and (very) light reading —pulp fiction, romance novels, and thrillers—are essential. In August we delight in the simple pleasure of shifting our gaze from the beach, to the sky, to a book in slow, lazy spirals.

Historically, pagans celebrated **Lammas** in the month of August. Lammas, meaning "loaf mass," is an old English festival celebrating the ripening of grains. Throughout the Middle Ages, it was an important marker on the wheel of the year; in addition to the grain harvest, it was also a time for holding fairs, paying rents, and electing officials. The grain harvest varies by region. In southern climates, rice and millet are harvested in August; in temperate climates, wheat; and in northern climates, the August harvest yields rye, barley, and oats. According to tradition, the grain crop was blessed and then baked into countless loaves. Since freshly baked bread is the centerpiece of the Lammas feast, the bread is broken and ritually offered to the four corners of the earth after reciting a humble blessing.

Lughnasa is an ancient, pre-Christian harvest festival that was mounted in August and closely resembled Lammas celebrations. Lughnasa is one of the four great Celtic festivals that divided the year. Dedicated to Lugh, the Celtic god of light, Lughnasa was a time to perform sacred harvest rituals and feast. Irish farmers took the first fruits of the corn harvest to a hilltop and buried it in the earth. Following a feast of newly harvested foods, the Irish mounted plays featuring a Lugh impersonator who banished the monster of famine and blight. Lughnasa was also a day for visiting wells, which were believed to be at the peak of their healing powers in August. People dipped their hands and toes into the water to cure their ailments before the arrival of winter. Blessings recited on this holiday celebrated the grain harvest and the glory of God.

In August, people pause in remembrance of the day on which the atom bomb was dropped in Hiroshima, Japan.

On **Hiroshima Day**, we are reminded of the terrible destruction—physical, emotional, and spiritual—that resulted from the release of the first atom bomb on August 6, 1945. On this day, people from around the world visit Sadako Sasaki's monument at the Hiroshima Peace Park in Japan. Sadako was two years old at the time of the bombing and was later diagnosed with leukemia, the "atom bomb disease." As a teenager, Sadako's best friend told her the Japanese legend that anyone who folds a thousand paper cranes is granted a wish. Sadako was only able to fold 644 paper cranes before her death in 1955; she wished to be able to run and play again. Since that time, people fold paper cranes and offer prayers of peace on Hiroshima Day.

Special Hiroshima Day ceremonies at Sadako's monument invite candlelight vigils and the recitation of simple songs and prayers. In some years, thousands gather to light candles and fold cranes while others sing songs evoking peace and compassion; Hiroshima Day is a time to collectively mourn and to be reminded of the sanctity of human life.

August sunsets—rich with dusty pinks, luminescent mauves, and fierce golds—are a feast for the eyes. Afterward, the nighttime stars enrich our late-night strolls along the beach or unlit country roads. Around August 11, the Perseids or "Night of the Shooting Stars" arrives and continues for several weeks in some parts of the world. Since the year 830, an annual meteor shower has originated from the constellation Perseus. When the shower reaches its peak, it can be seen everywhere except the South Pole. It is the perfect time to witness nature's fireworks and revel in the beauty of the majestic August sky.

By late August, our attention shifts from resting to preparing for fall. Back-to-school sales encourage us to purchase new clothes, shoes, and stationery, regardless of whether we are returning to school or not. For college students, August means time to pack up one's bags and return to campus. While clearing up our summer belongings, grains of sand—that cling to our tanned skin, beach towels, and shoes—trigger memories of a summer well spent.

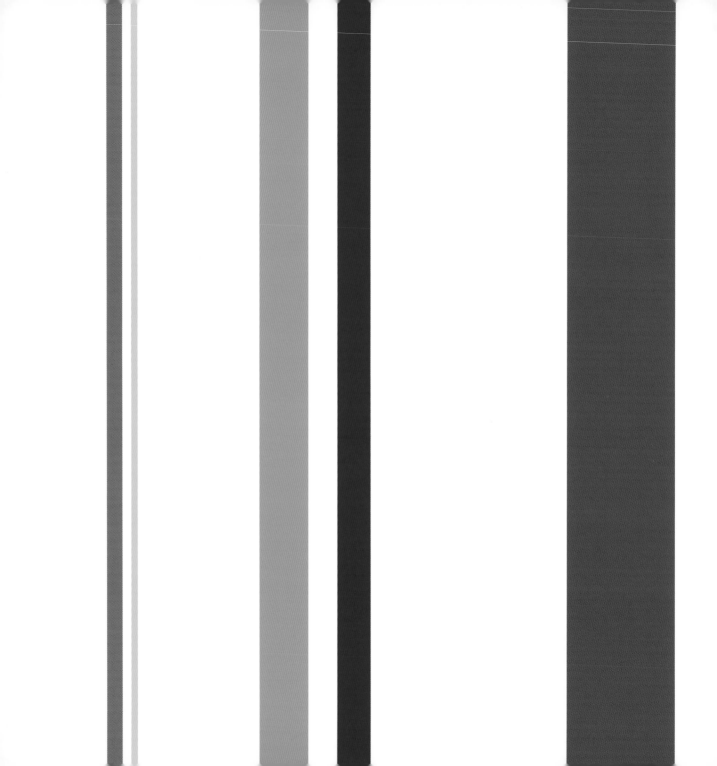

SELECTED SOURCES

Appelbaum, Diana Karter. *Thanksgiving: An American Holiday, an American History.* New York: Facts on File Publications, 1985.

Armstrong, Karen. *A History of God: The 4,000-Year Quest of Judaism, Christianity, and Islam.* New York: Ballantine Books, 1994.

Aveni, Anthony. *The Book of the Year: A Brief History of Our Seasonal Holidays.* New York: Oxford University Press, 2002.

Campanelli, Pauline. *Wheel of the Year: Living the Magical Life.* St. Paul, MN: Llewellyn Publications, 2000.

Du Bois, W. E. B. *The Souls of Black Folk.* New York: Bantam Books, 1989.

hooks, bell. *All About Love: New Visions.* New York: William Morrow & Company, 2000.

McGaa, Ed. *Mother Earth Spirituality: Native American Paths to Healing Ourselves and Our World.* San Francisco: HarperCollins Publishers, 1990.

Meyers, Miriam. *A Bite off Mama's Plate: Mothers' and Daughters' Connections to Food.* Westport, CT: Bergin & Garvey, 2001.

Muller, Wayne. *Sabbath: Restoring the Sacred Rhythm of Rest.* New York: Bantam Books, 1999.

Panati, Charles. *Panati's Extraordinary Origins of Everyday Things.* San Francisco: Perennial Currents, 1989.

Penner, Lucille Recht. *The Thanksgiving Book.* New York: Hastings House Book Publishers, 1986.

Pennick, Nigel. *The Pagan Book of Days: A Guide to the Festivals, Traditions, and Sacred Days of the Year.* Rochester, VT: Destiny Books, 1992.

Raboteau, Albert J. *Canaan Land: A Religious History of African Americans.* New York: Oxford University Press, 2001.

Ryan, M. J., ed. *A Grateful Heart: Daily Blessings for the Evening Meal from Buddha to the Beatles.* Berkeley, CA: Conari Press, 1994.

Steindl-Rast, Brother David. *Gratefulness, the Heart of Prayer: An Approach to Life in Fullness.* Ramsey, NJ: Paulist Press, 1984.

PERMISSIONS

Grateful acknowledgment is made to the authors and publishers for permission to excerpt from the following works:

Page 9: Excerpted from *The Mystic Heart: Discovering a Universal Spirituality in the World's Religions,* by Wayne Teasdale. Reprinted with permission from New World Library. www.newworldlibrary.com.

Pages 18, 54: Excerpts from *Gratefulness, the Heart of Prayer: An Approach to Life in Fullness* by Brother David Steindl-Rast. Copyright ©1984 by Brother David Steindl-Rast, Paulist Press, New York, Mahwah, NJ. Used with permission of Paulist Press. www.paulistpress.com.

Page 24: From *The Collected Poems of Langston Hughes* by Langston Hughes ©1994 by the Estate of Langston Hughes. Used by permission of Alfred A. Knopf, a division of Random House, Inc.

Page 29, 89, 121: From *The Upanishads* translated by Juan Mascaro. Copyright © 1965 by Juan Mascaro. Reprinted by permission of Penguin Books (UK), Ltd.

Pages 34, 51, 76, 97: *Wheel of the Year* by Pauline Campanelli © 1989. Llewellyn Worldwide, Ltd. PO Box 64383, St. Paul, MN 55164. All rights reserved, used by permission.

Page 61: From *Unseen Rain: Quatrains of Rumi,* translated by John Moyne and Coleman Barks. Copyright ©1986 by Coleman Barks. Reprinted by arrangement with Shambhala Publications, Inc., Boston, www.shambhala.com.

Page 66: Taken from *Reaching Out: The Three Movements of the Spiritual Life,* by Henri J. M. Nouwen. Copyright © 1998. Used by permission of The Zondervan Corporation.

Page 70: From *The Prophet* by Khalil Gibran. Copyright © 1923 by Khalil Gibran and renewed 1951 by Administrators C.T.A. of Kalhil Gibran Estate and Mary G. Gibran. Used by permission of Alfred A. Knopf, a division of Random House, Inc.

Page 79: Brief quotation as submitted from *The Essential Rumi,* translated by Coleman Barks. Translation copyright © 1997 by Coleman Barks. Reprinted by permission of author.

Page 83: From *The Collected Works of St. Teresa of Avila, Volume II.* Translated by Kieran Kavanaugh and Otilio Rodriguez. Copyright © 1980 by Washington Province of Discalced Carmelites ICS Publications 2131 Lincoln Road, N.E. Washington, D.C. 20002 U.S.A.

Page 83: Brief quotation reprinted by permission of Gloria Steinem, contributing editor at *Ms.* magazine.

Page 87: From *Hildegard of Bingen's Book of Divine Works with Music and Letters* by Hildegard of Bingen, edited by Matthew Fox. Copyright © 1987 by Bear and Company. Reprinted by permission of Bear and Company.

Page 88: Excerpt from www.gratefulness.org/*Sacred Journey* magazine, October 2001. Reprinted by kind permission of www.gratefulness.org.

Page 94: Reprinted with the permission of Scribner, an imprint of Simon & Schuster Adult Publishing Group, from *The Collected Works of W. B. Yeats, Volume 1: The Poems,* Revised, edited by Richard J. Finneran.

INDEX